Dr. Franklin, Dr. Scott

The immortal Mentor

Dr. Franklin, Dr. Scott

The immortal Mentor

ISBN/EAN: 9783337054786

Printed in Europe, USA, Canada, Australia, Japan

Cover: Foto ©ninafisch / pixelio.de

More available books at **www.hansebooks.com**

IMMORTAL MENTOR:

OR,

MAN's UNERRING GUIDE

TO A

HEALTHY, WEALTHY, AND HAPPY LIFE.

In three Parts.

BY

LEWIS CORNARO, Dr. *FRANKLIN,* and Dr. *SCOTT.*

" Reason's whole pleasure, all the joys of sense,
" Lie in three words—health, peace, and competence.
" Blest health consists with temperance alone,
" And peace, O virtue! peace is all thy own."

POPE.

PHILADELPHIA:

PRINTED FOR THE REV. MASON L. WEEMS,
BY FRANCIS AND ROBERT BAILEY,
NO. 116, HIGH-STREET.

1796.

The Great ADDISON, bestows the following eulogium on the Author of the first part of this work.

"*CORNARO* was of an infirm conſtitution till about forty, when, by obſtinately perſiſting in the Rules recommended in this Book, he recovered a perfect ſtate of health, inſomuch, that at four-ſcore he publiſhed this Treatiſe. He lived to give a fourth edition of it, and after having paſſed his hundredth year, died without pain or agony, like one who falls aſleep. This Book is highly extolled by many eminent authors, and is written with ſuch a ſpirit of cheerfulneſs and good ſenſe, as are the natural concomitants of temperance and virtue."

CONTENTS.

PART I.

	PAGE.
CHAP. I. *Man's* unerring Guide to a Long and Healthy Life	1
II. *The Method of Correcting a Bad Constitution*	41
III. *A Letter from Sig. Lewis Cornaro, to the Right Rev. Barbara, Patriarch of Aquileia*	52
IV. *Of the Birth and Death of Man*	62

APPENDIX.

CONTENTS.

PAGE.

APPENDIX. *Golden Rules of Health, selected from Hippocrates, Plutarch, and several other eminent Physicians and Philosophers* . 81

PART II.

INTRODUCTION . . . 97
The Way to Wealth . . 107
Advice to a Young Tradesman . . 126

PART III.

CHAP. I. *A sure Guide to Happiness* . . 133
II. *On Social Love* . . 234

THE IMMORTAL MENTOR, &c.

IT is an unhappiness into which the people of this age are fallen, that luxury is become fashonable and too generally preferred to frugality. Prodigality is now-a-days tricked up in the pompous titles of generosity and grandeur; whilst blest frugality is too often branded as the badge of an avaricious and sordid spirit.

This error has so far seduced us, as to prevail on many to renounce a frugal way of living, though taught by nature, and to indulge those excesses which serve only to abridge the number of our days. We are grown old before we have been able to taste the pleasures of being young. And the time which ought to be the summer of our lives is often the beginning of their winter.

Oh unhappy Italy! Doest thou not see, that gluttony and excess rob thee, every year, of more inhabitants than pestilence, war, and famine could have done? Thy true plagues, are thy numerous luxuries in which thy deluded citizens indulge themselves to an excess unworthy of the rational character, and utterly ruinous to their health. Put a stop to this fatal abuse, for God's sake, for there is not, I am certain of it, a vice more abominable in the eyes of the divine Majesty, nor any more destructive. How many have I seen cut off, in the flower of their days by this unhappy custom of high feeding! How many excellent friends has gluttony deprived me of, of, who, but for this accurfed vice, might have been an ornament to the world, an honour to their country, and have afforded me as much joy in their lives, as I now feel concern at their deaths.

In order, therefore, to put a ftop to fo great an evil, I have undertaken this little book, and I attempt it the more readily, as many young gentlemen have requefted it of me, moved thereto by feeing their fathers drop off in the flower of their youth, and me fo found and hearty at the age of eighty-one. They begged me to let them know by what means I attained to fuch excellent health and fpirits at my time of life. I could not but think their curiofity very laudable, and was willing to gratify them, and at the fame time do fome fervice to my countrymen, by declaring, in the firft place, what led me to renounce intemperance and lead a temperate life; fecondly, by fhewing the rules I obferved;
and

and thirdly, what unfpeakable fatisfaction and advantage I derived from it; whence it may be very clearly feen how eafy a thing it is for a wife man to efcape all the curfes of intemperance, and fecure to himfelf the ineftimable felicities of vigorous health and chearful age.

The firft thing that led me to embrace a temperate life, was, the many and fore evils which I fuffered from the contrary courfe of living; my conftitution was naturally weakly and delicate, which ought in reafon to have made me more regular and prudent, but being like moft young men, too fond of what is ufually called good eating and drinking, I gave the rein to my appetites. In a little time I began to feel the ill effects of fuch intemperance; for I had fcarce attained to my thirty-fifth year, before I was attacked with a complication of diforders, fuch as, head-achs, a fick ftomach, cholicky uneafineffes, the gout, rheumatic

rheumatic pains, lingering fevers, and continual thirſt; and though I was then but in the middle of my days, my conſtitution ſeemed ſo entirely ruined that I could hardly hope for any other termination to my ſufferings but death.

THE beſt phyſicians in Italy employed all their ſkill in my behalf, but to no effect. At laſt they told me, very candidly, that there was but one thing that could afford me a ſingle ray of hope, but one medicine that could give a radical cure, *viz.* the immediate adoption of a temperate and regular life. They added moreover, that, now, I had no time to loſe, that I muſt immediately, either chuſe a regimen or death, and that if I deferred their advice much longer, it would be too late for ever to do it. This was a home thruſt. I could not bear the thoughts of dying ſo ſoon, and being convinced of their abilities and experience, I thought the wifeſt courſe I could take, would be to follow their advice, how difagreeable foever it might feem.

I THEN requefted my phyficians to tell me exactly after what manner I ought to govern myfelf? To this they replied, that I fhould always confider myfelf as an infirm perfon; eat nothing but what agreed with me, and that in fmall quantity. I then immediately entered on this new courfe of life, and, with fo determined a refolution, that nothing has been fince able to divert me from it. In a few days I perceived that this new way of living agreed very well with me; and in lefs than a twelvemonth I had the unfpeakable happinefs to find that all my late alarming fymptoms were vanifhed, and that I was perfectly reftored to health.

No fooner had I began to tafte the fweets of this new refurrection, but I made many very pleafing reflections on the great advantage of temperance, and thought within myfelf, " if this virtue has

" had

" had fo divine an efficacy, as to cure me
" of fuch grievous diforders, furely it
" will help my bad conftitution and con-
" firm my health." I therefore applied
myfelf diligently to difcover what kinds
of food were propereft for me, and made
choice of fuch meats and drinks only as
agreed with my conftitution, obferving
it as an inviolable law with myfelf, *always
to rife with an appetite to eat more if I pleafed.* In a word, I entirely renounced intemperance, and made a vow to continue
the remainder of my life under the fame
regimen I had obferved : A happy refolution this! The keeping of which entirely cured me of all my infirmities. I never before lived a year together, without
falling once, at leaft, into fome violent illnefs ; but this never happened to me afterwards ; on the contrary, I have always
been healthy ever fince I was temperate.

I MUST not forget here to mention
a circumftance of confiderable confequence.

quence. I have been telling of a great, and to me, a moſt happy change in my way of living. Now all changes, tho' from the *worſt* to the *beſt* habits, are, at firſt, diſagreeable, I found it ſo; for having long accuſtomed myſelf to high feeding, I had contracted ſuch a fondneſs for it, that though I was daily deſtroying myſelf, yet did it, at firſt, coſt me ſome ſtruggle to relinquiſh it. Nature, long uſed to hearty meals, expected them, and was quite diſſatisfied with my moderate repaſts. To divert my mind from theſe little diſſatisfactions, I uſed immediately after dinner, to betake myſelf to ſome innocent amuſement or uſeful purſuit, ſuch as, my devotions, my book, muſic, &c.

But to return.—Beſides the two foregoing important rules about eating and drinking, that is, not to take of any thing, but as much as my ſtomach could eaſily digeſt, and to uſe thoſe things only which

which agreed with me. I have very carefully avoided all *extremes* of *heat* and *cold*, excessive fatigue, interruption of my usual time of rest, *late hours*, and *too close* and *intense thinking*. I am likewise greatly indebted for the excellent health I enjoy, to that calm and temperate state in which I have been careful to keep my passions.

THE influence of the passions on the nerves, and health of our bodies, is so great, that none can possibly be ignorant of it. He therefore who seriously wishes to enjoy good health, must, above all things, learn to conquer his passions, and keep them in subjection to reason. For let a man be never so temperate in diet, or regular in exercise, yet still some unhappy passion, if indulged to excess, will prevail over all his regularity, and prevent the good effects of his temperance; no words, therefore, can adequately express the wisdom of guarding

against

against an influence so destructive. Fear, anger, grief, envy, hatred, malice, revenge and despair, are known by eternal experience, to weaken the nerves, disorder the circulation, impair digestion, and often to bring on a long train of hysterical and hypochondriacal disorders; and extreme sudden fright, has often occasioned immediate death.

On the other hand, moderate joy, and all those affections of the mind which partake of its nature, as chearfulness, contentment, hope, virtuous and mutual love, and courage in doing good, invigorate the nerves, give a healthy motion to the fluids, promote perspiration, and assist digestion; but violent anger (which differs from madness only in duration) throws the whole frame into tempest and convulsion, the countenance blackens, the eyes glare, the mouth foams, and in place of the most gentle and amiable, it makes a man the most frightful and terrible

rible of all animals. The effects of this dreadful paſſion do not ſtop here; it never fails to create bilious, inflammatory, convulſive, and ſometimes apoplectic diſorders, and ſudden death.

Solomon was thoroughly ſenſible of the deſtructive tendencies of ungoverned paſſions, and has, in many places, cautioned us againſt them. He emphatically ſtyles " envy a rottenneſs of the " bones;" and ſays, that " wrath ſlay- " eth the angry man, and envy killeth " the ſilly one*;" and, " that the wick- " ed ſhall not live out half their days."

For

---

* The reader will I hope excuſe me for relating the following tragical anecdote, to confirm what the benevolent Cornaro has ſaid on the baneful effects of envy, &c.

In the city of York in England, there died ſome time ago, a young lady by the name of D——n. For five years before her death, ſhe appeared to be lingering and melancholy. Her fleſh withered away, her appetite decayed, her ſtrength failed, her feet could no longer ſuſtain her tottering emaciated body, and her diſſolution ſeemed at hand. One day ſhe called her intimate friends to her bed-ſide, and as well as ſhe could, ſpoke to the following effect:

For as violent gales of wind will soon wreck the strongest ships, so violent passions of hatred, anger, and sorrow, will soon destroy the best constitutions.

However, I must confess to my shame, that I have not been at all times so

"I know you all pity me, but alas! I am not worthy of your pity; for all my misery is entirely owing to the wickedness of my own heart. I have two sisters; and I have all my life been unhappy, for no other reason but because of their prosperity. When we were young, I could neither eat nor sleep in comfort, if they had either praise or pleasure. As soon as they were grown to be women, they married greatly to their advantage and satisfaction: this galled me to the heart; and though I had several good offers, yet thinking them rather unequal to my sisters, I refused them, and then was inwardly vexed and distressed, for fear I should get no better. I never wanted for any thing, and might have been very happy, but for this wretched temper. My sisters loved me tenderly, for I concealed from them as much as possible this odious passion, and yet never did any poor wretch lead so miserable a life as I have done, for every blessing they enjoyed was a dagger to my heart. 'Tis this Envy, which, preying on my very vitals, has ruined my health, and is now carrying me down to the grave. Pray for me, that God of his infinite mercy may forgive me this horrid sin; and with my dying breath I conjure you all, to check the first risings of a passion that has proved so fatal to me."

so much of a philosopher and Christian, as entirely to avoid these disorders: but I have reaped the benefit of knowing by my own repeated experience, that these malignant passions have in general a far less pernicious effect on bodies that are rendered firm and vigorous by temperance, than on those that are corrupted and weakened by gluttony and excess.

It was hard for me to avoid every extreme of heat and cold, and to live above all the occasions of trouble which attend the life of man; but yet these things made no great impression on the state of my health, though I met with many instances of persons who sunk under less weight both of body and mind.

There was in our family a considerable law-suit depending against some persons, whose might overcame our right. One of my brothers, and some of my relations, were so mortified and grieved on account of the loss of this suit, that they

they actually died of broken hearts. I was as senfible as they could be, of the great injuftice done us, but thank God, fo far from breaking my heart, it fcarcely broke my repofe. And I afcribe *their* fufferings and *my* fafety, to the difference of our living. Intemperance and floth had fo weakened their nerves, and broken their fpirits, that they eafily funk under the weight of misfortune. While temperance and active life had fo invigorated my conftitution, as to make me happily fuperior to the evils of this momentary life.

At feventy years of age, I had another experiment of the ufefulnefs of my regimen. Some bufinefs of confequence calling me into the country, my coach-horfes ran away with me; I was overfet and dragged a long way before they could ftop the horfes. They took me out of the coach with my head battered, a leg and an arm out of joint, and truly

truly in a very lamentable condition. As soon as they had brought me home, they sent for the physicians, who did not expect I could live three days: however, I was soon cured, to the great astonishment of the physicians, and of all those who know me.

I BEG leave to relate one more anecdote, as an additional proof what an impenetrable shield temperance presents against the evils of life.

ABOUT five years ago, I was over-persuaded to a thing, which had like to have cost me dear. My relations, whom I love, and who have a real tenderness for me; my friends, with whom I was willing to comply in any thing that was reasonable; lastly, my physicians, who were looked upon as the oracles of health, did all agree that I eat too little; that the nourishment I took was not sufficient for one of my years; that I ought not only to support nature, but likewise to increase

the

the vigour of it, by eating a little more than I did. It was in vain for me to reprefent to them, that nature is content with a little; that with this little I had enjoyed excellent health fo many years; that to me the habit of it was become a fecond nature; and that it was more agreeable to reafon, that as I advanced in years and loft my ftrength, I fhould rather *leſſen* than *increaſe* the quantity of my food, efpecially as the powers of the ftomach muft grow weaker from year to year. To ftrengthen my arguments, I urged thofe two natural and true proverbs; one, that he who would eat a great deal muft eat but little; that is eating little makes a man live long, he muft eat a great deal. The other proverb was, that what we leave, after making a hearty meal, does us more good than what we have eaten. But neither my proverbs nor arguments could filence their affectionate intreaties. Wherefore to pleafe

perfons

perſons who where ſo dear to me, I conſented to increaſe the quantity of food, but with too ounces only. So that, as before I had always taken but twelve ounces of ſolid food in the day, I now increaſed it to fourteen, and as before I drank but fourteen ounces of wine in the day, I now increaſed it to ſixteen. This increaſe had in eight days time ſuch an effect on me, that from being remarkably chearful and briſk, I began to be peeviſh and melancholy, and was conſtantly ſo ſtrangely diſpoſed, that I neither knew what to ſay to others, nor what to do with myſelf. On the twelfth day I was attacked with a moſt violent pain in my ſide, which held me twenty-two hours, and was followed by a violent fever which continued thirty-five days, without giving me a moment's reſpite. However God be praiſed, I recovered, though in my ſeventy-eighth year, and in the coldeſt ſeaſon of a very cold winter,

and

and reduced to a mere skeleton; and I am positive, that, next to GOD, I am most indebted to temperance, for my recovery. O how great is the evil of intemperance, which could, in a few days bring on me so severe an illness, and how glorious are the virtues of temperance, which could thus bear me up, and snatch me from the jaws of death! Would all men but live regularly and temperately, there would not be a tenth of that sickness which now makes so many melancholy families, nor any occasion for a tenth part of those nauseous medicines, which they are now obliged to swallow in order to carry off those bad humours with which they have filled their bodies by over eating and drinking.—To say the truth would every one of us but pay a becoming attention to the quantity and quality of what he eats and drinks, and carefully observe the effects it has upon him, he would soon become his own physician; and indeed the

the very beſt he could poſſibly have, for people's conſtitutions are as different as their faces; and it is impoſſible, in many very important inſtances, for the moſt ſkilful phyſicians to tell a man of obſervation, what would agree with his conſtitution ſo well as he knows himſelf. I am willing to allow that a phyſician may be ſometimes neceſſary; and in caſes of danger, the ſooner the better. But for the bare purpoſe of preſerving ourſelves in good health, there needs no better phyſic than a temperate and regular life. It is a ſpecific and natural medicine, which preſerves the man, how tender ſoever his conſtitution be, and prolongs his life to above a hundred years, ſpares him the pain of a violent death, ſends him quietly out of the world, when the radical moiſture is quite ſpent, and which, in ſhort, has all the properties that are fancied to be in potable
gold

gold, which a great many perſons have ſought after in vain.

But alas! moſt men ſuffer themſelves to be ſeduced by the charms of a voluptuous life. They have not courage enough to deny their appetites; and being over-perſuaded by their inclinations ſo far, as to think they cannot give up the gratification of them, without abridging too much of their pleaſures, they deviſe arguments to perſuade themſelves, that it is more eligible to live ten years leſs, than to be upon the reſtraint, and deprived of whatever may gratify their appetites. Alas! they know not the value of ten years of healthy life, in an age when a man may enjoy the full uſe of his reaſon, and turn all his wiſdom and experience to his own, and the advantage of the world. To inſtance only in the ſciences. 'Tis certain that ſome of the moſt valuable books now extant, were written in thoſe laſt ten

ten years of their authors lives, which fome men pretend to undervalue; let fools and villains undervalue life, the world would lofe nothing by them, die when they will. But it is a lofs indeed, when *wife* and *good* men drop into the grave; ten years of life to men of that character, might prove an ineftimable blefling to their families and country. Is fuch an one a prieft only, in a little time he might become a bifhop, and by living ten years longer, might render the moft important fervices to the world by his active diffemination of virtue and piety. Is he the aged parent of a family, then though no longer equal to the toils of younger years, yet by his venerable prefence and matured counfels, he may contribute more to the harmony and happinefs of his children, than all their labours put together. And fo with all others, whether in church or ftate, army or navy, who are advanced in years,

though

though not equal to the active exercises of youth, yet in consequence of their superior wisdom and experiences, their lives may be of more service to their country, than the lives of thousands of citizens. Some, I know, are so unreasonable as to say that it is impossible to lead such a regular life. To this I answer, Galen, that great physician, led such a life, and advised others to it as the best physic. *Plato, Cicero, Isocrates,* and a great many famous men of past and present times, have practised it, and thereby arrived to an extreme old age.

You will tell me that *Plato*, as sober a man as he was, yet affirmed, that it is difficult for a man in public life to live so temperately, being often in the service of the state, exposed to the badness of weather, to the fatigues of travelling, and to eat whatever he can meet with. This cannot be denied; but then I maintain, that these things will never hasten a man's a man's death, provided he accustoms himself to a frugal way of living. There is no man, in what condition soever but may keep from over-eating; and thereby happily prevent those distempers that are caused by excess. They who have the charge of public affairs committed to their trust, are more obliged to it than any others: where there is no glory to be got for their country, they ought not to sacrifice themselves: they should preserve themselves to serve it; and if they pursue my method, it is certain they would ward off the distempers which heat and cold and fatigues might bring upon them; or should they be disturbed with them it would be but very lightly.

It may likewise be objected, that if one who is well, is dieted like one that is sick, he will be at a loss about the choice of his diet, when any distemper comes upon him. To this I say, that nature, ever attentive to the preservation
of

of her children, teaches us how we ought to govern ourselves in such a case. She begins by depriving us so entirely of out appetites, that we can eat little or nothing. At that time, whether the sick person has been sober or intemperate, no other food ought to be used, but such as is proper for his condition; such as broth, jellies, cordials, barley-water, &c. When his recovery will permit him to use a more solid nourishment, he must take less than he was used to before his sickness; and notwithstanding the eagerness of his appetite, he must take care of his stomach, till he is perfectly cured. Should he do otherwise, he would overburden nature, and infallibly relapse into the danger he had escaped. But notwithstanding this, I dare aver, that he who leads a sober and regular life, will hardly ever be sick; or but seldom, and for a short time. This way of living preserves us from those bad humours which

which occasion our infirmities, and by consequence heals us of all those distempers which they occasion. I do not pretend to say that every body must eat exactly as little as I do, or abstain from fruit, fish, and other things from which I abstain, because such dishes disagree with me. They who are not disordered by such dishes, are under no obligation to abstain from them. But they are under the greatest obligations to feed moderately, even on the most innocent food, since an overloaded stomach cannot digest.

It signifies nothing to tell me that there are several, who, though they live very irregularly, yet enjoy excellent health and spirits, and to as advanced an age, as those who live ever so soberly. For this argument is founded on such uncertainty and hazard, and occurs so seldom, as to look more like a miracle than the regular work of nature. And those, thofe, who, on the credit of their youth and *conftitution*, will pay any regard to fo idle an objection, may depend on it, that they are the betrayers and ruiners of their own health.

And I can confidently and truly affirm, that an old man, even of a bad conftitution, who leads a regular and fober life, is furer of a longer one, than a young man of the beft conftitution who lives diforderly. All therefore who have a mind to live long and healthy, and die without ficknefs of body or mind, muft immediately begin to live temperately, for fuch a regularity keeps the humours of the body mild and fweet, and fuffers no grofs fiery vapours to afcend from the ftomach to the head; hence the brain of him who lives in that manner enjoys fuch a conftant ferenity, that he is always perfectly mafter of himfelf. Happily freed from the tyranny of bodily appetites and paffions, he
eafily

easily soars above, to the exalted and delightful contemplation of heavenly objects; by this means his mind becomes gradually enlightened with divine truth, and expands itself to the glorious enrapturing view of the Power, Wisdom, and Goodness of the Almighty. —He then descends to nature, and acknowledges her for the fair daughter of GOD, and views her varied charms with sentiments of admiration, joy, and gratitude, becoming the most favoured of all sublunary beings. He then clearly discerns, and generously laments the wretched fate of those who will not give themselves the trouble to subdue their passions; and those three most ensnaring lusts, the lust of the flesh, the lust of honours, and the lust of riches, which all wise and good men have firmly opposed and conquered, when they passed through this mortal state; for knowing such passions to be inconsistent with reason

son and happiness, they at once nobly broke through their snares, and applied themselves to virtue and good works, and so became men of good and sober lives. And when in process of time, and after a long series of years, they see the period of their days drawing nigh, they are neither grieved nor alarmed. Full of acknowledgments for the favours already received from GOD, they throw themselves into the arms of his future mercy. They are not afraid of those dreadful punishments, which they deserve who have shortened their days by guilty intemperance. They die without complaining, sensible that they did not come into this world to stay for ever, but are pilgrims and travellers to a far better. Exulting in this faith, and with hopes big with immortality, they go down to the grave in a good old age, enriched with virtues, and laden with honours.

And they have the greater reafon not to be dejected at the thought of death, as they know it will not be violent, feverifh or painful. Their end is calm, and they expire, like a lamp when the oil is fpent, without convulfion or agony, and fo they pafs gently away, without pain or ficknefs, from this earthly and corruptible to that celeftial and eternal life, whofe happinefs is the reward of the virtuous.

O holy, happy, and thrice bleffed temperance! how worthy art thou of our higheft efteem! and how infinitely art thou preferable to an irregular and diforderly life! Nay, would men but confider the effects and confequences of both, they would immediately fee, that there is as wide a difference between them, as there is betwixt light and darknefs, heaven and hell. Some there are who tell us that old age is no bleffing, that when a man is paft feventy, his life is nothing but weakness, infirmity, and misery. But I can assure these gentlemen, they are mightily mistaken; and that I find myself, old as I am, (which is much beyond what they speak of) to be in the most pleasant and delightful stage of life.

To prove that I have reason for what I say, they need only enquire how I spend my time, what are my usual employments; and to hear the testimony of all those that know me. They unanimously testify, that the life I lead, is not a dead and languishing life, but as happy a one as can be wished for in this world.

They will tell you, that I am still so strong at fourscore and three, as to mount a horse without any help or advantage of situation; that I can not only go up a single flight of stairs, but climb a hill from bottom to top, a-foot, and with the greatest ease; that I am always

always merry, always pleafed, always in humour; maintaining a happy peace in my own mind, the fweetnefs and ferenity whereof appear at all times in my countenance.

Besides, they know that it is in my power to pafs away the time very pleafantly; having nothing to hinder me from tafting all the pleafures of an agreeable fociety, with feveral perfons of parts and worth. When I am willing to be alone, I read good books, and fometimes fall to writing; feeking always an occafion of being ufeful to the public, and doing fervice to private perfons, as far as poffible. I do all this without the leaft trouble; and in fuch times as I fet apart for thefe employments.

I dwell in a houfe, which, befides its being fituated in the pleafanteft part of *Padua*, may be looked on as the moft convenient and agreeable manfion in that

that city. I there make me apartments proper for the winter and fummer, which ferve as a fhelter to defend me from the extreme heat of the one, and the rigid coldnefs of the other. I walk out in my gardens, along my canals and walks; where I always meet with fome little thing or other to do, which, at the fame time, employs and amufes me.

I SPEND the months of *April*, *May*, *September*, and *October*, at my country-houfe, which is the fineft fituation imaginable: the air of it is good, the avenues neat, the gardens magnificent, the waters clear and plentiful; and this feat may well pafs for an inchanted palace.

SOMETIMES I take a walk to my *Villa*, all whofe ftreets terminate at a large fquare; in the midft of which is a pretty neat church, and large enough for the bignefs of the parifh.

THROUGH

Through this *Villa* runs a rivulet; and the country about it is enriched with fruitful and well cultivated fields; having at prefent a confiderable number of inhabitants. This was not fo formerly: It was a marfhy place, and the air fo unwholfome, that it was more proper for frogs and toads, than for men to dwell in. But on my draining off the waters, the air mended, and people reforted to it fo faft, as to render the place very populous; fo that I may, with truth, fay, that I have here dedicated to the Lord, a church, altars, and hearts to worfhip him; a circumftance this, which affords me infinite fatisfaction as often as I reflect on it.

It is with great fatisfaction that I fee the end of a work of fuch importance to this state, I mean that of draining and improving fo many large tracts of uncultivated ground, a work which I never expected to have feen completed; but,

but, thank GOD, I have lived to fee it, and was even in perfon in thefe marfhy places, along with the commiffaries, for two months together, during the heats of fummer, without ever finding myfelf the worfe for the fatigues I underwent. Of fuch wonderful efficacy is that temperate life which I conftantly obferve.

IF in difcourfing on fo important a fubject as this, it be allowable to fpeak of trifles, I might tell you, that at the age of fourfcore and three, a temperate life had preferved me in that fprightlinefs of thought, and gaiety of humour, as to be able to compofe a very entertaining comedy, highly moral and inftructive, without fhocking or difgufting the audience; an evil too generally attending our comedies, and which it is the duty, and will be the eternal honor of the magiftracy to difcountenance and fupprefs, fince nothing has a more fatal tendency to corrupt the morals

rals of youth, than such plays as abound with wanton allusions, and wicked sneers and scoffs on religion and matrimony.

As an addition to my happiness, I see myself immortalized as it were, by the great number of my descendants. I meet with, on my return home, not only two or three, but eleven grand-children, all blest with high health, sweet dispositions, bright parts, and of promising hopes. I take a delight in playing with the little pratlers; those who are older I often set to sing and play for me on instruments of music.—Call you this an infirm crazy old age, as they pretend, who say, that a man is but half alive after he is seventy? They may believe me if they please, but really I would not exchange my serene chearful old age, with any one of those young men, even of the best constitution, who give the loose to their appetites; knowing as I do, that they are thereby subjecting

themselves

themselves every moment to disease and death.

I REMEMBER all the follies of which I was guilty in my younger days, and am perfectly sensible of the many and great dangers they exposed me to. I know with what violence young persons are carried away by the heat of their blood. They presume on their strength, just as if they had taken a sure lease of their lives: and must gratify their appetites whatever it cost them, without considering that they thereby feed those ill humours, which do most assuredly hasten the approach of *sickness* and *death;* two evils, which of all others are the most unwelcome and terrible to the wicked. The first of these, *sickness*, is highly unwelcome, because it effectually stops their career after this world's business and pleasures, which being their sole delight and happiness, must be inexpressibly sad and mortifying. And the impatience

tience and gloom of sickness is rendered tenfold more insupportable to them, because it finds them utterly destitute of those pious affections, which alone can soothe the severity of sickness and charm the pangs of pain. They had never cultivated an acquaintance with God, nor accustomed themselves to look up to him as to a merciful Father, who sends affliction to wean us from this scene of vanity. They had never, by prayers and good works, endeavoured to secure his friendship, or cherish that love which would make his dispensations welcome. So that unblest with these divine consolations, the season of sickness must be dark and melancholy indeed; and besides all this, their hearts often sink within them at the prospect of DEATH, that ghastly king of terrors, who comes to cut them off from all their dear delights in this world, and send their unwilling souls to suffer the punishment which

which their own guilty confcience tells them is due to their wicked lives.

But from thefe two evils, fo dreadful to many, bleffed be God, I have but little to fear; for, as for *death*, I have a joyful hope that that change, come when it may, will be glorioufly for the *better;* and befides, I truft, that He whofe divine voice I have fo long obeyed, will gracioufly fupport and comfort his aged fervant in that trying hour. And as for *ficknefs*, I feel but little apprehenfion on that account, fince by my divine medicine TEMPERANCE, I have removed all the caufes of illnefs; fo that I am pretty fure I fhall never be fick, except it be from fome intent of *Divine* mercy, and then I hope I fhall bear it without a murmur, and find it for my good. Nay I have reafon to think that my foul has fo agreeable a dwelling in my body, finding nothing in it but peace and harmony between
my

my reafon and fenfes, that fhe is very well pleafed with her prefent fituation; fo that I truft I have ftill a great many years to live in health and in fpirits, and enjoy this beautiful world, which is indeed beautiful to thofe who know how to make it fo, as I have done, and likewife expect (with God's affiftance) to be able to do in the next.

Now fince a regular life is fo happy, and its bleffings fo permament and great, all I have ftill left to do, (fince I cannot accomplifh my wifhes by force) is to befeech every man of found underftanding to embrace, with open arms, this moft valuable treafure of a long and healthy life; a treafure, which, as it far exceeds all the riches of this world, fo it deferves above all things to be diligently fought after, and carefully preferved. This is that divine fobriety, fo agreeable to the Deity, the friend of nature, the daughter of reafon, and the fifter sister of all the virtues. From her, as from their proper root, spring life, health, chearfulness, industry, learning, and all those employments worthy of noble and generous minds. She is the best friend and safest guardian of life; as well of the rich as of the poor; of the old as of the young. She teaches the rich modesty; the poor frugality; men continence; women chastity; the old, how to ward off the attacks of death; and bestows on youth, firmer and securer hopes of life. She preserves the senses clear, the body light, the understanding lively, the soul brisk, the memory tenacious, our motions free, and all our faculties in a pleasing and agreeable harmony.

O MOST innocent and divine sobriety! the sole refreshment of nature, the nursing mother of life, the true physic of soul as well as of body. How ought men to praise thee for thy princely gifts, for thy incomparible bleſſings! But as no man is able to write a ſufficient panegyric on this rare and excellent virtue, I ſhall put an end to this diſcourſe, left I ſhould be charged with exceſs in dwelling ſo long on ſo pleaſing a ſubject. Yet as numberleſs things may ſtill be ſaid of it, I leave off with an intention to ſet forth the reſt of its praiſes at a more convenient opportunity.

CHAP. II.

THE METHOD OF CORRECTING A BAD CONSTITUTION.

I WAS born with a very choleric, haſty diſpoſition; flew into a paſſion for the leaſt trifle, huffed every body about me, and was ſo intolerably diſagreeable, that many perſons of gentle manners abſolutely

lutely shunned my company. On discovering how great an injury I was doing myself, I at once resolved to make this vile temper give way to reason. I considered that a man overcome by passion, must at times, be no better than a madman, and that the only difference between a passionate and a madman, is, that the one has lost his reason for ever, and the other is deprived of it by fits only; but that in one of these, though never so short, he may do some deed of cruelty or death, that will ruin his character, and destroy his peace *for ever*. A sober life, by cooling the fever of the blood, contributed much to cure me of this frenzy; and I am now become so moderate, and so much a master of my passion, that no body could perceive that it was born with me.

It is true indeed, the most temperate may sometimes be indisposed, but then they have the pleasure to think that it

is

is not the effect of their own vices; that it will be but moderate in its *degree*, and of short continuance.

MANY have said to me, *" How can you, when at a table covered with a dozen delicious dishes content yourself with one dish, and that the plainest too at the table? It must surely be a great mortification to you, to see so many charming things before you, and yet scarcely taste them."* This question has frequently been put to me, and with an air of surprize. I confess it has often made me unhappy; for it proves that such persons are got to such a pass, as to look on the gratification of their appetites as the highest happiness, not considering that the mind is properly the man, and that it is in the affections of a virtuous and pious mind, a man is to look for his truest and highest happiness. When I sit down, with my eleven grand-children, to a table covered with various dainties, of which, for the sake of of a light easy stomach, I may not, at times, chuse to partake, yet this is no mortificaton to me; on the contrary, I often find myself most happy at these times. How can it otherwise than give me great delight when I think of that goodness of GOD, which blesses the earth with such immense stores of good things for the use of mankind; and which, over and above all this goodness, has put me into the way of getting such an abundance of them for my dear grand-children; and, besides must it not make me very happy to think that I have gotten such a mastery over myself as never to abuse any of those good things, but am perfectly contented with such a portion of them as keeps me always in good health. O what a triumph of joy is this to my heart! What a sad thing it is that young people will not take instruction, nor get benefit from those who are older and wiser than themselves!

themselves! I may use, in this matter, the words of the wise man, "I have seen all things that are done under the sun." I know the pleasures of eating, and I know the joys of a virtuous mind, and can say from long experience, that the one excelleth the other as far as light excelleth darkness; the one are the pleasures of a mere animal, the other those of an angel.

Some are so thoughtless as to say, that they had rather be afflicted twice or thrice a year with the gout, and other distempers, than deny themselves the pleasure of eating and drinking to the full of such things as they like; that for their part they had rather eat and drink as they like, though it should shorten their lives, that is, "give them a short life and a merry one." It is really a surprising and *sad* thing, to see reasonable creatures, so ready to swallow the most dangerous absurdities. For how

how, in the name of common sense, can the life of a glutton or a sot be a merry one? If men could eat to excess, drink to fillness, and rust in sloth, and after all, suffer no other harm than the abridgement of ten or a dozen years of life, they might have some little excuse for calling it a merry life, though surely it could appear so to none but persons of a sadly vitiated taste. But since an intemperate life will assuredly sow in our bodies the seeds of such diseases as will, after a few short years of feverish pleasure, make life a burthen to us, with what face can any reasonable being call this a merry life?

O sacred and most bountiful Temperance! how greatly am I indebted to thee for rescuing me from such fatal delusions; and for bringing me, through the divine benediction, to the enjoyment of so many felicities, and which, over and above all these favours conferred

red on thine old man, haft fo ftrengthened his ftomach, that he has now a better relifh for his dry bread than he had formerly for the moft exquifite dainties, fo that, by eating little, my ftomach is often craving after the manna, which I fometimes feaft on with fo much pleafure, that I fhould think I trefpaffed on the duty of temperance, did I not know that one muft eat to fupport life; and that one cannot ufe a plainer or more natural diet.

My fpirits are not injured by what I eat, they are only revived and fupported by it. I can, immediately on rifing from table, fet myfelf to write or ftudy, and never find that this application, though fo hurtful to hearty feeders, does me any harm; and, befides, I never find myfelf drowfey after dinner, as a great many do;—the reafon is, I feed fo temperately, as never to load my ftomach nor opprefs my nerves, fo
that

that I am always as light, active, and chearful after meals as before.

O thou vile wicked intemperance, my sworn enemy, who art good for nothing but to murder those who follow thee; how many of my dearest friends hast thou robbed me of, in consequence of their not believing me! But thou hast not been able to destroy me according to thy wicked intent and purpose. I am still alive in spite of thee, and have attained to such an age, as to see around me eleven dear grand-children, all of fine understandings, and amiable dispositions, all given to learning and virtue; all beautiful in their persons and lovely in their manners, whom, had I not abandoned thee thou infamous source of corruption, I should never have had the pleasure to behold. Nor should I enjoy those beautiful and convenient apartments which I have built from the ground, with such highly improved gardens,

dens, as required no small time to attain their present perfection. No, thou accursed hag, thy nature is to impoverish and destroy those who follow thee. How many wretched orphans have I seen embracing dunghills; how many miserable mothers, with their helpless infants, crying for bread, while their deluded fathers, slaves to thy devouring lusts, were wasting their substance in rioting and drunkenness!

But thou art not content with consuming the substance, thou wouldest destroy the very families of those who are so mad as to obey thee. The temperate poor man who labours hard all day, can boast a numerous family of rosy cheeked children, while thy pampered slaves, sunk in ease and luxury, often languish without an heir to their ample fortunes. But since thou art so pestilential a vice, as to poison and destroy the greatest part of mankind, I am determined to use my utmost endeavours to extirpate thee, at least in part. And I promise myself, that my dear grandchildren will declare eternal war against thee, and following my example, will let the world see the blessedness of a temperate life, and so expose thee, O cruel intemperance! for what thou really art, a most wicked, desperate, and mortal enemy of the children of men.

It is really a very surprising and sad thing to see persons grown to men's estate, and of fine wit, yet unable to govern their appetites, but tamely submitting to be dragged by them into such excesses of eating and drinking, as not only to ruin the best constitutions, and shorten their lives, but eclipse the lustre of the brightest parts, and bury themselves in utter contempt and uselessness. O what promising hopes have been shipwrecked, what immortal honours have been sacrificed at the shrine of low sensuality;

fuality; Happy, thrice happy, thofe who have early been inured to habits of felf-denial, and taught to confider the gratification of their appetites as the unfailing fource of difeafes and death. Ye generous parents who long to fee your children adorned with virtue, and beloved as the benefactors of their kind; O teach them the unfpeakable worth of felf government. Unfupported by this, every advantage of education and opportunity will avail them but little: though the hiftory of ancient worthies, and the recital of their illuftrious deeds, may at times kindle up in their bofoms a flame of glorious emulation, yet alas! this glow of coveted virtue, this flufh of promifed honor, is tranfient as a gleam of winter funfhine; foon overfpread and obfcured by the dark clouds of fenfuality.

CHAP. III.

CHAP. III.

A LETTER FROM SIGNIOR LEWIS CORNARO TO THE RIGHT REVEREND BARBARO, PATRIARCH OF AQUILEIA.

My Lord,

WHAT thanks do we not owe to the divine goodnefs, for this wonderful invention of writing, whereby we can eafily communicate to our abfent friends, whatever may afford them pleafure or improvement! By means of this moft welcome contrivance, I fhall now endeavour to entertain you with matters of the greateft moment. It is true indeed, that what I have to tell you is no news,—but I never told it you at the age of *ninety-one.* Is it not a charming thing, that I am able to tell you, that my health and ftrength are in fo excellent a state,

state, that, instead of diminishing with my age, they seem to increase as I grow old? All my acquaintance are surprised at it; but I, who know the cause of this singular happiness, do every where declare it. I endeavour, as much as in me lies, to convince all mankind, that a man may enjoy a paradise on earth even after the age of four-score.

Now my Lord, I must tell you, that within these few days past, several learned Doctors of this University came to be informed by me, of the method I take in my diet, having understood that I am still healthful and strong; that I have my senses perfect; that my memory, my heart, my judgment, the tone of my voice, and my teeth, are all as sound as in my youth; that I write seven or eight hours a day, and spend the rest of the day in walking out a-foot, and in taking all the innocent pleasures that are
allowed

allowed to a virtuous man; even music itself in which I bear my part.

Ah, Sir! how sweet a voice would you perceive mine to be, were you to hear me, like another *David*, chant forth the praises of God to the sound of my Lyre! You would certainly be surprised and charmed with the harmony which I make. Those gentlemen particularly admired, with what easiness I write on subjects that require both judgment and spirit.

They told me, that I ought not to be looked on as an old man, since all my employments were such as were proper for a youth, and did by no means resemble the works of men advanced in years; who are capable of doing nothing after fourscore, but loaded with infirmities and distempers, are perpetually languishing in pain, not half so chearful, pleasant and happy as I am.

Several

SEVERAL phyficians were fo good as to prognofticate to me, ten years ago, that it was impoffible for me to hold out three years longer: however, I ftill find myfelf lefs weak than ever, and am ftronger this year than any that went before. This fort of miracle, and the many favours which I received from GOD, obliged them to tell me, that I brought along with me at my birth, an extraordinary and fpecial gift of nature; and for the proof their opinion, they employed all their rhetoric, and made feveral elegant fpeeches on that head. It muft be acknowledged, my Lord, that eloquence has a charming force on the mind of man, fince it often perfuades him to believe that which never was, and never could be. I was very much pleafed to hear them difcourfe; and could it be helped, fince they were men of parts who harangued at that rate? But that which delighted me moft,

was

was to reflect, that age and experience may render a man wifer than all the colleges in the world can. And it was in truth by their help, that I knew the error of that notion. To undeceive thofe gentlemen, and at the fame time fet them right, I replied, that their way of arguing was not juft: that the favour I received was no fpecial, but a general and univerfal one: that I was but a man as well as others: that we have all judgment and reafon, which the Creator has beftowed on us to preferve our lives: that man, when young, being more fubject to fenfe than reafon, is too apt to give himfelf up to pleafure; and that when arrived to thirty or forty years of age, he ought to confider, that, if he has been fo imprudent as to lead, till that time, a diforderly life, it is now high time for him to take up and live temperately; for he ought to remember, that though he has hitherto been held up by the vigour of

youth

youth and a good conſtitution, yet he is now at the noon of life, and muſt bethink himſelf of going down towards the grave, with a heavy weight of years on his back, of which his frequent pains and infirmities are certain forerunners ; and that therefore, if he has not been ſo happy as to do it already, he ought now, immediately to change his courſe of life.

I MUST confeſs, it was not without great reluctance that I abandoned my luxurious way of living. I began with praying to GOD, that he would grant me the gift of Temperance, well knowing that he always hears our prayers with delight. Then, confidering, that when a man is about to undertake any thing of importance, he may greatly ſtrengthen himſelf in it, by often looking forward to the great pleaſures and advantages that he is to derive from it. Juſt as the huſbandman takes comfort under his toils, by reflecting on the ſweets of abundance ;

dance; and as the good chriftian gladdens in the fervice of GOD, when he thinks on the glory of that fervice, and the eternal joys that await him; fo I, in like manner, by ferioufly reflecting on the innumerable pleafures and bleffings of health, and befeeching GOD to ftrengthen me in my good refolutions, immediately entered on a courfe of temperance and regularity. And though it was at firft highly difagreeable, yet I can truly fay, that in a very little time, the difagreeablenefs vanifhed, and I came to find great delight in it.

Now on hearing my arguments, they all agreed that I had faid nothing but what was reafonable; nay, the youngeft among them told me, that he was willing to allow that thefe advantages might be common to all men, but was afraid, they were feldom attained; and that I muft be fingularly favoured of Heaven to get above the delights of an eafy life,

and

and embrace one quite contrary to it; that he did not look on it to be impossible, since my practice convinced him of the contrary, but however, it seemed to him to be very difficult.

I REPLIED, that it was a shame to relinquish a good undertaking on account of the difficulties that might attend it, and that the greater the difficulty, the more glory should we acquire: that it is the will of the Creator, that every one should attain to a long life, because in his old age, he might be freed from the bitter fruits that were produced by sense, and might enjoy the good effects of his reason; that when he shakes hands with his vices, he is no longer a slave to the devil, and finds himself in a better condition of providing for the salvation of his soul: that GOD, whose goodness is infinite, has ordained that the man who comes to the end of his race, should end his life without any distemper, and so

pass.

pafs, by a sweet and easy death, to a life of immortality and glory, which I expect. I hope (said I to him) to die singing the praises of my Creator. The sad reflection, that we must one day cease to live, is no disturbance to me, though I easily preceive, that at my age, that day cannot be far off; nor am I afraid of the terrors of hell, because, blessed be GOD, I have long ago shaken hands with my sins, and put my trust in the mercy and merits of the blood of *Jesus Christ*.

To this my young antagonist had nothing to say, only that he was resolved to lead a sober life, that he might live and die as happily as I hoped to do; and that though hitherto he had wished to be young a long time, yet now he desired to be quickly old, that he might enjoy the pleasures of such an admirable age.

SOME

Some sensual persons give out, that I have troubled myself to no purpose, in composing a treatise concerning temperance, and that I have lost my time in endeavouring to persuade men to the practice of that which is impossible. Now this surprises me the more, as these gentlemen must see that I had led a temperate life many years before I composed this treatise, and that I never should have put myself to the trouble of composing it, had not long experience convinced me, that it is a life which any man may easily lead, who really wishes to be healthy and happy. And, besides the evidence of my own experience, I have the satisfaction to hear, that numbers on seeing my treatise have embraced such a life, and enjoyed from it the very same blessings which I enjoy. Hence, I conclude, that no man of good sense will pay any regard to so frivolous an objection. The truth is, those gentlemen

tlemen who make this objection, are so unhappily wedded to the poor pleasure of eating and drinking, that they cannot think of moderating it, and as an excuse for themselves, they choose to talk at this extravagant rate. However, I pity these gentlemen with all my heart, though they deserve for their intemperance, to be tormented with a complication of distempers, and to be the victims of their passions a whole eternity.

CHAP. IV.

OF THE BIRTH AND DEATH OF MAN.

THAT I may not be deficient in that duty of charity, which all men owe to one another, or lose one moment of that pleasure which conscious usefulness nefs affords; I again take up my pen. What I am going to fay will be looked on as impoffible, or incredible; but nothing is more certain, nor more worthily to be admired by all pofterity. I am now ninety-five years of age, and find myfelf as healthy and brifk, as if I were but twenty-five.

WHAT ingratitude fhould I be guilty of, did I not return thanks to the divine Goodnefs, for all his favors conferred upon me? Moft of your old men have fcarce arrived to fixty, but they find themfelves loaded with infirmities: they are melancholy, unhealthful; always full of the frightful apprehenfions of dying: they tremble day and night for fear of being within one foot of their graves; and are fo ftrongly poffeffed with the dread of it, that it is a hard matter to divert them from that doleful thought. Bleffed be GOD, I am free from their ills and terrors. It is my opinion, that I ought

not

not to abandon myself to that vain fear: this I will make appear by the sequel.

Some there are, who bring along with them a strong constitution into the world, and live to old age: but it is generally (as already observed) an old age of sickness and sorrow; for which they are to thank themselves; because they most unreasonably presume on the strength of their constitution; and will not on any account, abate of that hearty feeding which they indulged in their younger days. Just as if they were to be as vigorous at fourscore as in the flower of their youth; nay, they go about to justify this their imprudence, pretending that as we lose our health and vigor by growing old, we should endeavour to repair the loss, by increasing the quantity of our food, since it is by sustenance that man is preserved.

But in this they are dangerously mistaken; for as the natural heat and strength

strength of the stomach lessens as a man grows in years, he should diminish the quantity of his meat and drink, common prudence requiring that a man should proportion his diet to his digestive powers.

This is a certain truth, that sharp sour humours on the stomach, proceed from a slow imperfect digestion; and that but little good chyle can be made, when the stomach is filled with fresh food before it has carried off the former meal. —It cannot therefore be too frequently, nor too earnestly recommended, that as the natural heat decays by age, a man ought to abate the quantity of what he eats and drinks; nature requiring but very little for the healthy support of the life of man, especially that of an old man. Would my aged friends but attend to this single precept which has been so signally serviceable to me, they would not be troubled with one twentieth of those infirmities which now harrafs and make their lives fo miferable. They would be light, active, and chearful like me, who am now near my *hundredth year*. And thofe of them who were born with good conftitutions, might live to the age of one hundred and twenty. Had I been bleft with a robuft conftitution, I fhould in all probability, attain the fame age. But as I was born with feeble ftamina, I fhall not perhaps outlive an hundred. And this moral certainty of living to a great age is to be fure, a moft pleafing and defirable attainment, and it is the prerogative of none but the temperate. For all thofe who (by immoderate eating and drinking) fill their bodies with grofs humours, can have no reafonable affurance of living a fingle day longer : oppreffed with food and fwoln with fuperfluous humours, they are in continual danger of violent fits of the cholic, deadly ftrokes of the apoplexy, fatal attacks of the cholera

cholera morbus, burning fevers, and many such acute and violent diseases, whereby thousands are carried to their graves, who a few hours before looked very hale and hearty. And this moral certainty of long life is built on such good grounds as seldom ever fail. For, generally speaking, Almighty GOD seems to have settled his works on the sure grounds of natural causes, and temperance is (by divine appointment) the natural cause of health and long life. Hence it is next to impossible, that he who leads a strictly temperate life, should breed any sickness or die of an unnatural death, before he attains to the years to which the natural strength of his constitution was to arrive. I know some persons are so weak as to excuse their wicked intemperance, by saying, that " the race is not always to the swift, nor the battle to the strong," and that therefore, let them eat and drink as they please, they shall

not

not die till their time comes. How fcandaloufly do thefe men mifunderftand Solomon and abufe truth! How would it ftartle us to hear our friends fay, " that let them fleep and play, as they pleafe, they fhall not be beggars till their time comes."

Solomon does indeed fay, that " the race is not always to the fwift, nor the battle to the ftrong;" but he muft be no better than a madman, who thence infers, that it is not *generally* fo. For the invariable and eternal experience of mankind demonftrates, that ninety-nine times in an hundred, the race is to the fwift, and the battle to the ftrong, bread to the induftrious, and health to the temperate.

But it is a matter of fact, and not to be denied, that, though temperance has the divine efficacy to fecure us from violent difeafe and unnatural death, yet it is not to be fuppofed to make a man immortal. It

is

is impoſſible but that time, which effaces all things, ſhould likewiſe deſtroy that moſt curious workmanſhip of GOD, the human body: but it is man's privilege to end his days by a natural death, that is, without pain and agony, as they will ſee me, when the heat and ſtrength of nature is quite exhauſted. But I promiſe myſelf, that day is a pretty comfortable diſtance off yet, and I fancy I am not miſtaken, becauſe I am ſtill healthy and briſk, reliſh all I eat, ſleep quietly, and find no defect in any of my ſenſes. Beſides, all the faculties of my mind are in the higheſt perfection; my underſtanding clear and bright as ever; my judgment ſound; my memory tenacious; my ſpirits good; and my voice, the firſt thing that fails others, ſtill ſo ſtrong and ſonorous, that every morning and evening, with my dear grand-children around me, I can addreſs my prayers and chant the praiſes of the Almighty. O, how

glorious

glorious this life of mine is like to be, replete with all the felicities which man can enjoy on this side of the grave; and exempt from that sensual brutality which age has enabled my better reason to banish, and therewith all its bitter fruits, the extravagant passions and distressful perturbations of mind. Nor yet can the fears of death find room in my mind as I have no licensed sins, to cherish such gloomy thoughts: neither can the death of relations and friends give me any other grief than that of the first movement of nature, which cannot be avoided, but is of no long continuance. Still less am I liable to be cast down by the loss of wordly goods. I look on these things as the property of heaven; I can thank him for the loan of so many comforts, and when his wisdom sees fit to withdraw them, I can look on their departure without murmuring.—This is the happiness of those only, who grow old

old in the ways of temperance and virtue; a happiness which seldom attends the most flourishing youth who live in vice. Such are all subject to a thousand disorders, both of body and mind, from which I am entirely free: on the contrary, I enjoy a thousand pleasures, which are as pure as they are calm.

The first of these is to do service to my country. O! what a glorious amusement, in which I find infinite delight, in shewing my countrymen how to fortify this our dear city of Venice, in so excellent a manner, as to make her a famous republic, a rich and matchless city. Another amusement of mine is, that of shewing this maid and queen of cities, in what manner she may always abound with provisions, by manuring untilled lands, draining marshes, and laying under water, and thereby fattening fields, which had all along been barren for want of moisture. My third amusement amufement is in fhewing my native city, how, though already ftrong, fhe may be rendered much ftronger; and, tho' extremely beautiful, may ftill increafe in beauty; though rich, may acquire more wealth, and may be made to enjoy better air, though her air is excellent. Thefe three amufements, all arifing from the idea of public utility, I enjoy in the higheft degree. Another very great comfort I enjoy is, that having been defrauded when young, of a confiderable eftate, I have made ample amends for that lofs, by dint of thought and induftry, and without the leaft wrong done to any perfon, have doubled my income, fo that I am able not only to provide for my dear grand-children, but to educate and affift many poor youth to begin the world. And I cannot help faying, I reflect with more pleafure on what I lay out in that way, than in any other.

ANOTHER

Another very confiderable addition to my happinefs is, that what I have written from my own experience, in order to recommend *temperance*, has been of great ufe to numbers, who loudly proclaim their obligations to me for that work, feveral of them having fent me word from foreign parts, that, under God, they are indebted to me for their lives. But that which makes me look on myfelf as one of the happieft of men, is, that I enjoy as it were, two forts of lives; the one terreftrial, which I poffefs in fact; the other celeftial, which I poffefs in thought; and this thought is attended with unutterable delight, being founded on fuch glorious objects, which I am morally fure of obtaining, through the infinite goodnefs and mercy of God. Thus I enjoy this terreftrial life, partly through the beneficent influences of temperance and fobriety, virtues fo pleafing to heaven; and I enjoy, through cordial love of the fame divine Majesty, the celestial life, by contemplating so often on the happiness thereof, that I can hardly think of any thing else. And I hold, that dying in the manner I expect, is not really death, but a passage of the soul from this earthly life, to a celestial, immortal, and infinitely perfect existence. And I am so far charmed with the glorious elevation to which I think my soul is designed, that I can no longer stoop to those trifles, which, alas! charm and infatuate too great a part of mankind. The prospect of parting with my favourite enjoyments of this life, gives me but little concern; on the contrary, I thank God, I often think of it with secret joy, since by that loss I am to gain a life incomparably more happy.

O! who then would be troubled, were he in my place? what good man, but must instantly throw off his load of
wordly

worldly forrow, and addrefs his grateful homage to the Author of all this happinefs? However, there is not a man on earth, who may not hope for the like happinefs, if he would but live as I do. For indeed I am no angel, but only a man, a fervant of GOD, to whom a good and temperate life is fo pleafing, that even in this world he greatly rewards thofe who practife it.

AND whereas many embrace a holy and contemplative life, teaching and preaching the great truths of religion, which is *highly* commendable, the chief employment of fuch being to lead men to the knowledge and worfhip of GOD. O that they would likewife betake themfelves entirely to a regular and temperate life! They would then be confidered as faints indeed upon earth, as thofe primitive chriftians were, who obferved fo conftant a temperance, and lived fo long. By living like them, to the age of one hundred

hundred and twenty, they might make such a proficiency in holiness, and become so dear to God, as to do the greatest honour and service to the world; and they would besides, enjoy constant health and spirits, and be always happy within themselves; whereas they are now too often infirm and melancholy. If indeed they are melancholy, because they see God, (after all his goodness) so ungratefully requitted; or because they see men (notwithstanding their innumerable obligations to love) yet hating and grieving each other: such melancholy is truly amiable and divine.

But to be melancholy on any other account, is, to speak the truth, quite unnatural to good christians; such persons being the servants of God and heirs of immortality; and it is still more unbecoming the ministers of religion, who ought to consider themselves, as of all others,

others, in the moſt important, serviceable, and delightful employment.

I know, many of theſe gentlemen think that God does purpoſely bring theſe occaſions of melancholy on them that they may in this life do penance for their former ſins; but therein, as I think, they are much miſtaken. I cannot conceive, how God, who loves mankind, can be delighted with their ſufferings. He deſires that mankind ſhould be happy, both in this world and the next; he tells us ſo in a thouſand places in his word, and we actually find that there is not a man on earth, who does not feel the good Spirit of God, forbidding and condemning thoſe wicked courſes, which would rob him of that happineſs. No; it is the devil and ſin which bring all the evils we ſuffer, on our heads, and not God, who is our Creator and Father, and deſires our happineſs: his commands tend to no other purpose. And temperance would not be a virtue, if the benefit it does us by preserving us from distempers, were repugnant to the designs of God in our old age.

In short, if all religious people were strictly temperate and holy, how beautiful, how glorious a scene should we then behold! Such numbers of venerable old men as would create surprise. How many wise and holy teachers to edify the people by their wholesome preaching and good examples! How many sinners might receive benefit by their fervent intercessions! How many blessings might they shower upon the earth! and not as now, eating and drinking so intemperately, as to inflame the blood and excite worldly passions, pride, ambition, and concupiscence, soiling the purity of their minds, checking their growth in holiness, and in some unguarded moment, betraying them

them into fins difgraceful to religion, and ruinous to their peace for life.— Would they but feed temperately, and that chiefly on vegetable food, they would as I do, foon find it the moft agreeable, (by the cool temperate humours it affords) the beft friend to virtuous improvement, begetting gentle manners, mild affections, purity of thought, heavenly mindednefs, quick relifh of virtue, and delight in GOD. This was the life led by the holy fathers of old, who fubfifted entirely on vegetables, drinking nothing but pure water, and yet lived to an extreme old age, in good health and fpirits, and always happy within themfelves. And fo may all in our days live, provided they would but mortify the lufts of a corruptible body, and devote themfelves entirely to the exalted fervice of GOD; for this is indeed the privilege of every faithful chriftian as Jefus Chrift left it,

when

when he came down upon earth to shed his precious blood, in order to deliver us from the tyrannical servitude of the devil; and all through his immense goodness.

To conclude, since length of days abounds with so many blessings, and I am so happy as to have arrived at that state, I find myself bound (in charity) to give testimony in favour of it, and solemnly assure all mankind, that I really enjoy a great deal more than what I now mention; and that I have no other motive in writing on this subject, than to engage them to practise, all their lives, those excellent virtues of temperance and sobriety, which will bring them, like me, to a happy old age. And therefore I never cease to raise my voice, crying out to you, my friends, may your days be many, that you may long serve GOD, and be fitter for the glory which he prepares for his children!

APPEN-

APPENDIX.

GOLDEN RULES

OF

HEALTH,

SELECTED FROM HIPPOCRATES, PLUTARCH, AND SEVERAL OTHER EMINENT PHYSICIANS AND PHILOSOPHERS.

OF all the people on the face of the earth, the Americans are under the greateſt obligations to live temperatly. Formed for commerce, our country abounds with bays, rivers and creeks, the exhalations from which, give the air a dampneſs unfriendly to the ſprings of life. To counteract this infelicity of climate,

mate, reason teaches us to adopt every measure that may give tone and vigor to the constitution. This precaution, at all times necessary, is peculiarly so in autumn, for then the body is relaxed by the intense heat of the dog-days, the air is filled with noxious vapours from putrid vegetables; Nature herself wears a sickly, drooping aspect; the most robust feel a disagreeable weariness and soreness of their flesh, a heaviness and sluggishness in motion, quick feverish flushings, and sudden chills darting along their nerves, (all plain proofs of a sickly atmosphere, and tottering health). Now, if ever, we need the aid of all-invigorating temperance, now keep the stomach light and vigorous by moderate feeding, the veins well stored with healthy blood, and the nerves full braced by manly exercise and comely chearfulness. Be choice of your diet, fruit perfectly ripe, vegetables thoroughly done, and

meats

meats of the eafieft digeftion, with a glafs or two of generous wine at each meal, and all taken in fuch prudent moderation, as not to load but ftrengthen the conftitution. For at this critical juncture, a fingle act of intemperance, which would fcarcely be felt in the wholefome frofts of winter, often turns the fcale againft nature, and brings on obftinate indigeftion, load at ftomach, lofs of apetite, a furred tongue, yellownefs of eyes, bitter tafte in the mouth in the morning, bilious vomitings, agues, fevers, &c. which in fpite of the beft medicines, often wear a man away to a ghoft. If bleffed with a good conftitution, he *may* perhaps crawl on to *winter*, and get braced up again by her friendly frofts; but if old or infirm, it is likely death will overtake him, before he can reach that city of refuge.

" THE giddy practice of throwing afide our winter clothes too early in the fpring, spring, and that of expofing our bodies, when overheated, to fudden cold, has deftroyed more people, than famine, peftilence and fword."*—*Sydenham.*

Those who, by any accident, have loft a meal, (fuppofe their dinner) ought not to eat a plentiful fupper; for it will lie heavy on their ftomach, and they will have a more reftlefs night than if they had both dined and fupped heartily. He therefore, who has miffed his dinner, fhould

---

* I saw (fays an American officer) thirteen grenadiers lying dead by a fpring, in confequence of drinking too freely of the cold water, while dripping with fweat in a hard day's march, in fummer. And many a charming girl, worthy of a tenderer hufband, has funk into the icy embraces of death, by fuddenly expofing her delicate frame, warm from the ball-room, to the cold air. And fince " the univerfal caufe acts not by partial, but by general laws," many a good foul, with more piety than prudence, turning out quite warm from a crowded preaching into the cold air without cloak or furtout, has gone off in a galloping confumption to that happy world, where pain and ficknefs are unknown. What a melancholy thing it is, that people cannot take care of their fouls, without neglecting their bodies, nor feek their falvation without ruining their health!

should make a light supper of spoon victuals, rather than of any strong solid food." *Hippocrates.*

He who has taken a larger quantity of food than usual, and feels it heavy and troublesome on his stomach, will, if he is a wise man, go out and puke it up immediately*. *Hippocrates.*

And here I cannot omit mentioning a a very ruinous error into which too many are fond of running, I mean, the frequent use of strong vomits and purgatives. A man every now and then feeds too freely on some favourite dish; by such excess the stomach is weakened, the

body

---

* The wise son of Sirach confirms this precept, and says, Ecclef. xxxi. 21. "If thou hast been forced to eat, arise, go forth and puke, and thou shalt have rest." And most certain it is, (adds an ingenious physician) that hundreds and thousands have brought sickness and death on themselves, by their ignorance or neglect of this rule. But at the same time people should carefully avoid a repetition of that excess, which renders such an evacuation necessary, for frequent vomitings do greatly tend to weaken and destroy the tone of the stomach.

body filled with superfluous humours, and he presently finds himself much out of sorts. The only medicine in this case, is moderate exercise, innocent amusement, and a little abstinence, this is nature's own prescription, as appears by her taking away his appetite. But having long placed his happiness in eating and drinking, he cannot think of relinquishing a gratification so dear to him, and so sets himself to force an appetite by drams, slings, elixir of vitriol, wine and bitters, pickles, sauces, &c. and on the credit of this artificial appetite, feeds again as if he possessed the most vigorous health. He now finds himsef *entirely* disordered, general heaviness and weariness of body, flatulent uneasiness, frequent eructations, loss of appetite, disturbed slumbers, frightful dreams, bitter taste in the mouth, &c. He now complains of a foul stomach, or (in his own words) that his stomach is full of bile; and immediately takes

takes a dofe of tartar emetic or a ftrong purgative, to cleanfe out his ftomach, and fo prepare for another courfe of high living. Of all the Apollyons or deftroyers of nerves, health and life, this is the greateft; and I have no fort of doubt on my own mind but it has broken down more conftitutions, brought on more diftempers, and fent more people to an early grave, than all the vices of this bedlam world put together. How much wifer would it be in this cafe to follow the advice of the celebrated Bœrhaave, i. e. to ufe a little abftinence, take moderate exercife, and thereby help nature to carry off her crudities and recover her fprings. I have been often told by a lady of quality, whofe circumftances obliged her to be a good œconomift, and whofe prudence and temperance preferved her health and fenfes unimpaired to a great age, that fhe had kept herfelf out of the hands of the phyficians many years by
this

this fimple reigmen. People in health fhould never force themfelves to eat when they have no appetite; Nature, the beft judge in thefe matters, will never fail to let us know the proper time of refrefhment. To act contrary to this rule, will affuredly weaken the powers of digeftion, impair health and fhorten life. *Plutarch.*

" LET us beware of fuch food as tempts us to eat when we are not hungry, and of fuch liquors as entice us to drink when we are not thirfty." *Socrates.*

IT is really furprifing (fays Plutarch) what benefit men of letters would receive from reading aloud every day; we ought therefore to make that exercife familiar to us, but it fhould not be done immediately after dinner, nor fatigue, for that error has proved hurtful to many. But though loud reading is a very healthy exercife, violent vociferation is highly dangerous; it has in thoufands

fands of inftances burft the tender blood veffels of the lungs, and brought on incurable confumptions*.

"The world has long made a juft diftinction betwixt men of learning, and wife men. Men of learning are ofttimes the weakeft of men: they read and meditate inceffantly, without allowing proper relaxation or refrefhment to the body; and think that a frail machine can bear fatigue as well as an immortal

---

* Would to God, all minifters of religion (I mention *them* becaufe they are generally moft wanting in this great article of prudence) would but attend to the advice of this eminent Philofopher. They would, many of them, live much longer, and confequently ftand a good chance to be more ufeful men here on earth, and brighter faints in heaven. What can give greater pain to a man who has the profperity of religion at heart, than to fee an *amiable, pious young divine*, (who promifed great fervices to the world) fpitting up his lungs, and dying of a confumption brought on by preaching ten times louder than he had need! Since the world began, no man ever fpoke with *half* the energy which the interefts of eternal fouls deferve, but there is a wide difference betwixt an *inftructive, moving, melting eloquence*, and a *loud, unmeaning monotony*.

mortal spirit. This puts me in mind of what happened to the camel in the fable; which, refusing though often premonished, to ease the ox in due time of a part of his load, was forced at last to carry not only the ox's whole load, but the ox himself also, when he died under his burden. Thus it happens to the mind which has no compassion on the body, and will not listen to its complaints, nor give it any rest, until some sad distemper compels the mind to lay study and contemplation aside; and to lie down, with the afflicted body, upon the bed of languishing and pain. Most wisely, therefore, does Plato admonish us to take the same care of our bodies as of our minds; that like a well matched pair of horses to a chariot, each may draw his equal share of weight. And when the *mind* is most intent upon virtue and usefulness, the *body* should then be most cherished by prudence and

and temperence, that so it may be fully equal to such arduous and noble pursuits."—*Plutarch*.

Nothing is more injurous to health than hard study at night; it is inverting the order of nature, and ruining the constitution.

But most of all, it is improper to lie reading in bed by candle light; for it not only partakes of the usual inconveniences of night study, such as straining the eyes, weakening the sight, fatiguing the mind, and wearing away the constitution, but is oft-times the cause of the saddest calamities; thousands of elegant houses, with all their costly furniture, have been reduced to ashes by this very imprudent practice.

But how can giddy youth, hurried on by strong passions and appetites, be prevented from running into those excesses, which may cut them off in the prime of their days, or at least hoard up

diseases

diseases and remorse for old age? Why, their passions and appetites must early be restrained by proper discipline and example. This important office must be done by their parents, whose first and greatest care should be " to train up their children in the way they should go, that when they are old they may not depart from it."

" O that parents (says the excellent Mr. Locke) would carefully instil into their children that great principle of all virtue and worth, viz. nobly to deny themselves every wrong desire, and steadily follow what reason dictates as best, though the appetite should lean the other way. We often see parents by humouring them when little, corrupt the principles of virtue in their children; and wonder afterwards to taste the bitter waters of their undutifulness or wickedness, when they themselves have contributed thereto. Why should we wonder

wonder that he who has been accuſtomed to have his will in every thing, when he was in coats, ſhould deſire and contend for it when he is in breeches? Youth is the golden ſeaſon to inure the mind to the practice of virtue, on which their future health and reſpectability depend, and without which it will be impoſſible to deliver their conſtitutions, unbroken, to manhood and old age. Vice is utterly inconſiſtent with health, which can never dwell with lewdneſs, luxury, ſloth and violent paſſions. The life of the epicure and rake, is not only ſhort, but miſerable. It would ſhock the modeſt and compaſſionate, to hear of thoſe exquiſite pains, and dreadful agonies, which profligate young perſons ſuffer from their debaucheries, before they can even reach the friendly ſhelter of an untimely *grave*. Or if ſome few ſtop ſhort in their career of riot, before they have quite deſtroyed the ſprings of life, yet thoſe ſprings are

generally

generally rendered so feeble and crazy, by the liberties which they have already taken, that they only support a gloomy, dispirited, dying life, tedious to themselves, and troublesome to all around them; and (which is still more pitiable) often transmit their complaints to an innocent unhappy offspring."

PART II.

THE WAY TO WEALTH,

BY

DOCTOR FRANKLIN.

INTRODUCTION.

> " But for one end, one much neglected use, are riches
> " worth your care:
> " This noble end is—to shew the virtues in their fair-
> " est light;
> " To make humanity the minister of *bounteous Provi-*
> " *dence,*
> " *And teach the breast the generous luxury of doing good."*
>
> Dr. ARMSTRONG.

THERE is scarcely among the evils of life, any so generally dreaded as poverty. Many other kinds of misery a man may easily forget, because they do not always force themselves upon his regards. But it is impossible to pass a day or an hour, in the company of men without seeing how much poverty is exposed to neglect and insult; and in its lowest *state, to hunger and nakedness;*

nakedneſs; to injuries, againſt which, every paſſion is in arms; and to wants, which nature, without the aids of religion, cannot ſuſtain.

Of theſe calamities, mankind in general ſeem to be ſenſible. We hear on every ſide the noiſe of trade; and ſee the ſtreets thronged with numberleſs multitudes, whoſe faces are clouded with anxiety, and whoſe ſteps are hurried by precipitation, from no other motive than the hope of gain. The whole world is put in motion by the deſire of that wealth, which is chiefly to be valued as it ſecures us from poverty and its miſeries. But there are always ſome whoſe paſſions or follies lead them to a conduct widely different from the general practice of mankind. I mean the thoughtleſs and the negligent, who, from an exceſs of careleſſneſs, or the ſeductions of company, indulge habits of pleaſure and expence above their fortunes; and thus miſpend their time, or waſte the inheritance of

their

their fathers, without ever seeming to reflect on the great sacrifice they are making, or the gulph to which they approach, till poverty, like an unexpected winter, comes upon them with all its chilling calamities, and awakens them to a pungent sense of their folly and wretchedness. The young, and those of the most generous and unsuspecting tempers, often fall into this evil net, out of which they seldom escape without suffering injuries, which they painfully feel and seriously lament through life. No man had a heart more disposed to pity, nor a head more able to counsel these unfortunates, than the sage Dr. FRANKLIN, the friend of man, and the great economist of AMERICA. His little work, entitled, " THE WAY TO WEALTH," is universally considered as a master-piece, on the art of making and preserving a fortune. But before we give the Reader a sight of this, we will exhibit to his view some of the many felicities of wealth, that

on

on seeing how much happiness he may derive from it to himself, and how many services he may therewith confer on others, he may apply with vigor and perseverance to the means conducive to so desireable an end.

In the first place—WEALTH always commands respect, unless its owner be an infamous wretch indeed; and even in that deplorable case, it has the magic powers of charity, to cover and hide a multitude of sins. It gives a man an air of consequence, and like true beauty, without any exertion of its own, wins the favour of all beholders. When the rich man goes into company, every body rise up to salute him: no features too hard to assume a smile; no back so stiff but can afford him a bow. He is placed in the uppermost seat at the table, and men covet to direct their conversation to him. The poor man speaketh, but no one regardeth: the rich openeth

openeth his mouth, and lo! silence is kept.

WHAT can be more pleasing to a man than to see himself thus honoured by his friends? But besides this satisfaction, which to the good, is very exquisite; it has a very happy moral effect on the mind. In a mind possessed of common sensibility, it must kindle the soft fire of good humour, and good humour naturally inspires benevolence and affection. Whence we infer, that a rich man, who is prudent, stands a much fairer chance to be good humoured than the poor, whose poverty exposes them to such frequent slights and neglects.

IN the second place—WEALTH places a man in a state which all must covet; a state of INDEPENDENCE. To owe no man any thing; to be able to go withersoever we please; and to face any company without dread of dunning, is a luxury too divine, even to be conceived by any who have not been haunted and hag ridden by creditors.

creditors. Say, ye debtors, ye poorest of mankind, say, ye who cannot look at a creditor without confusion, nor hear the name of justice without a pang; who startle at the sound of a shaken leaf, as though the feet of the sheriff were at the door, and fly as the murderer flies from the avenger of blood, whose sorrowful days are wasted in meditating fruitless plans of payment, while your midnight slumbers are frightened by dreams of bankruptcy, and apparitions of merciless creditors, sales, and houseless children: say, wherein is the life of a debtor better than the life of a dog. Are not the prospects of independence as reviving to your hearts, as the prospects of paradise to souls that have long pined in purgatory?

But, on the other hand, never to go in debt; or, if accident should render a trifling debt necessary; to have at home more than enough to defray it; to receive a creditor with a smiling countenance; to delight

light his eyes with the promised gold, and to dismiss him charmed with our punctuality and honour: Must not this, to a good man, afford a series of satisfactions, too complicated for detail, and too exquisite for description?

In the third place—WEALTH enables us to enjoy the purest and sublimest pleasures that are to be found on earth—the pleasures of doing good.

To a tender parent, the interests of his children are dear, as the blood which feeds the fountain of life. When he looks at them, his bowels are moved within him, because he remembers the evils which await them; He considers that ignorance leaves them an easy prey to the crafty and cruel; and that want betrays them to dishonesty and falsehood. Happy the parent who possesses wealth; he places before his children the lamp of knowledge, and they perceive the snares of the artful; he surrounds them with the blessings of competence, and they

they despise the gains of iniquity. He has sisters and brothers, perhaps, poor in worldly goods, but whom he loves as his own soul; and young relatives, whose little strong embraces, kindle all the parent within him. Is there on earth a happiness equal to that which he feels in supplying their wants; giving them education, and thus leading them, as by the hand, to usefulness and honour?

To welcome the weeping widow; to provide for her a place of rest; to dry up her tears; to feed and educate her little orphans, and to put them in a way to gain an honest livelihood.

To take by the hand poor young tradesmen; to lend them money; to set them up, and thus to enable them to be very useful to the community, and to make comfortable livings for themselves.

To build in the neighbourhoods of the poor, places of public worship, where the people

people may learn the knowledge of GOD, *and the happiness of a good life.*

To assist in providing houses where the sick and aged poor, who are not able to work for themselves, may be taken in, and have medicines and physicians to cure their sicknesses, and food and cloathing to make the remainder of their days happy.

To feel for a tenant's misfortunes, and to abate something of his rent in a bad season.

To silence the excuses of a poor debtor with a " well, well; don't be uneasy on account of this trifle; I know you are an honest man, and I am willing to wait till you can make it convenient to pay me."

THESE *are some of the numberless luxuries of beneficence which wealth enables a good man to enjoy. If you would enjoy them, listen to the instructions of* Dr. FRANKLIN, *and let the words of his mouth sink deep into your heart. Despise them not for their simplicity; for simple and unlearned is the multitude to which they are addressed.*

THE
WAY to WEALTH.

COURTEOUS READER,

I HAVE heard, that nothing gives an author fo great pleafure, as to find his works refpectfully quoted by others. Judge, then, how much I muft have been gratified by an incident I am going to relate to you. I ftopped my horfe, lately, where a great number of people were collected at an auction of merchant's goods. The hour of the fale not being come, they were converfing on the badnefs of the times; and one of the company called to a plain, clean

old

old man, with white locks, " Pray, father, Abraham, what think you of the times? Will not thefe heavy taxes quite ruin the country? How fhall we be ever able to pay them? What would you advife us to?"—Father Abraham, ftood up, and replied, " If you would have my advice, I will give it you in fhort; " for a word to the wife is e-nough," as Poor Richard fays." They joined in defiring him to fpeak his mind, and gathering round him, he proceeded as follows:

" Friends, fays he, the taxes are, indeed, very heavy; and, if thofe laid on by the government, were the only ones we had to pay, we might more eafily difcharge them; but we have many others, and much more grievous to fome of us. We are taxed twice as much by our idlenefs, three times as much by our pride, and four times as much by our folly; and from thefe

taxes

taxes the commissioners cannot ease or deliver us, by allowing an abatement. However, let us hearken to good advice, and something may be done for us; God helps them that help themselves," as Poor Richard says.

I. "It would be thought a hard government that should tax its people one-tenth part of their time, to be employed in its service: but idleness taxes many of us much more; sloth, by bringing on diseases, absolutely shortens life. " Sloth, like rust, consumes faster than labour wears, while the used key is always bright," as Poor Richard says. " But dost thou love life, then do not squander time, for that is the stuff life is made of," as Poor Richard says. How much more than is necessary do we spend in sleep? forgetting that " The sleeping fox catches no poultry, and that there will be sleeping enough in the grave," as Poor Richard says.

"If

"If time be of all things the most precious, wasting time must be," as Poor Richard says, " the greatest prodigality ;" since, as he elsewhere tells us, " Lost time is never found again; and what we call time enough always proves little enough :" Let us then up and be doing, and doing to the purpose; so by diligence shall we do more with less perplexity. " Sloth makes all things difficult, but industry all easy; and, he that riseth late, must trot all day, and shall scarce overtake his business at night; while laziness travels so slowly, that poverty soon overtakes him. Drive thy business, let not that drive thee; and early to bed and early to rise, makes a man healthy, wealthy, and wise," as Poor Richard says.

" So what signifies wishing and hoping for better times? We may make these times better, if we bestir ourselves. " Industry need not wish, and he that
lives

lives upon hope will die fasting. There are no gains without pains; then, help hands for I have no lands," or if I have they are smartly taxed. " He that hath a trade, hath an estate; and he that hath a calling, hath an office of profit and honour," as Poor Richard says; but then the trade must be worked at, and the calling well followed, or neither the estate nor the office will enable us to pay our taxes. If we are industrious, we will never starve; for at the working man's house, hunger looks in, but dares not enter." Nor will the bailiff or the constable enter, for " Industry pays debts, while despair increaseth them." What, though you have found no treasure, nor has any rich relation left you a legacy, " Diligence is the mother of good luck, and God gives all things to industry. Then plough deep, while sluggards sleep, and you shall have corn to sell and to keep."

Work

Work while it is called to-day, for you know not how much you may be hindered to-morrow. "One to-day is worth two to-morrows," as Poor Richard fays; and farther, "Never leave that till to-morrow, which you can do to-day." If you were a fervant, would you not be afhamed that a good mafter fhould catch you idle? Are you then your own mafter? be afhamed to catch yourfelf idle, when there is fo much to be done for yourfelf, your family, your relations, and your country. Handle your tools without mittens: remember, that "The cat in gloves catches no mice," as Poor Richard fays. It is true, there is much to be done, and, perhaps, you are weak-handed; but ftick to it fteadily, and you will fee great effects; for "Conftant dropping wears away ftones; and by diligence and patience the moufe ate in two the cable; and little ftrokes fell great oaks."

"Methinks

"Methinks I hear some of you say, "Must a man afford himself no leisure?" I will tell thee my friend what Poor Richard says; "Employ thy time well, if thou meanest to gain leisure; and, since thou art not sure of a minute, throw not away an hour." Leisure is time for doing something useful; this leisure the diligent man will obtain, but the lazy man never; for, "A life of leisure and a life of laziness are two things. Many, without labour would live by their wits only, but they break for want of stock;" whereas industry gives comfort, and plenty, and respect. "Fly pleasures, and they will follow you. The diligent spinner has a large shift; and now I have a sheep and a cow, every body bids me good-morrow."

II. "But with our industry, we must likewise be steady, settled, and careful, and oversee our own affairs with our own eyes, and not truſt too much to others; for, as Poor Richard ſays,

"I never ſaw an oft-removed tree,
Nor yet an oft-removed family,
That throve ſo well as thoſe that ſettled be."

" And again, " Three removes is as bad as a fire;" and again, " Keep thy ſhop, and thy ſhop will keep thee;" and again, " If you would have your buſineſs done, go; if not, ſend." And again,

"He that by the plough would thrive,
Himſelf muſt either hold or drive."

" And again, " The eye of a maſter will do more work than both his hands;" and again, " Want of care does us more damage than want of knowledge;" and again, " Not to overſee workmen, is to leave them your purſe open." Truſting too much to others care is the ruin of many; for, " In the affairs of this world, men are ſaved, not by faith, but by the want of it;" but a man's

own

own care is profitable; for, "If you would have a faithful servant, and one that you like, serve yourself. A little neglect may breed great mischief; for want of a nail the shoe was lost; for want of a shoe the horse was lost; and for want of a horse the rider was lost," being overtaken and slain by the enemy; all for want of a little care about a horse-shoe nail.

III. "So much for industry my friends, and attention to one's own business; but to these we must add frugality, if we would make our industry more certainly successful. A man may, if he knows not how to save as he gets, "keep his nose all his life to the grindstone, and die not worth a groat at last. A fat kitchen makes a lean will;" and

" Many estates are spent in the getting,
Since women for tea forsook spinning & knitting,
And men for punch forsook hewing and splitting."

"If you would be wealthy, think of saving, as well as of getting. The Indies

dies have not made Spain rich, becaufe her outgoes are greater than her incomes."

"Away, then, with your expenfive follies, and you will not then have fo much caufe to complain of hard times, heavy taxes, and chargeable families; for

"Women and wine, game and deceit,
Make the wealth fmall, and the want great."

And farther, "What maintains one vice, would bring up two children." You may think, perhaps, that a little tea, or a little punch now and then, diet a little more coftly, cloaths a little finer, and a little entertainment now and then, can be no great matter; but remember many a little makes a mickle." Beware of little expences; "A fmall leak will fink a great fhip," as Poor Richard fays; and again, "Who dainties love, fhall beggars prove?" and moreover, "Fools make feafts, and wife men eat them." Here you are all got together to this fale of fineries and

nick-

nick-nacks. You call them goods; but if you do not take care, they will prove evils to some of you. You expect they will be sold cheap, and, perhaps, they may for less than they cost; but, if you have no occasion for them, they must be dear to you. Remember what Poor Richard says, " Buy what thou hast no need of, and ere long thou shalt sell thy necessaries." And again, " At a great pennyworth pause a while:" he means, that perhaps the cheapness is apparent only, and not real; or the bargain, by straitening thee in thy business, may do the more harm than good. For in another place he says, " Many have been ruined by buying good pennyworths." Again, " It is foolish to lay out money in a purchase of repentance;" and yet this folly is practised every day at auctions, for want of minding the Almanack. Many a one, for the sake of finery on the back, have

gone

gone with a hungry belly, and half starved their families; " Silks and sattins, scarlet and velvets, put out the kitchen fire," as Poor Richard says. These are not the necessaries of life, they can scarcely be called the conveniencies: and yet only because they look pretty, how many want to have them? By these and other extravagancies, the genteel are reduced to poverty, and forced to borrow of those whom they formerly despised, but who, thro' industry and frugality, have maintained their standing; in which case it appears plainly, that a ploughman on his legs is higher than a gentleman on his knees," as Poor Richard says. Perhaps they have had a small estate left them, which they knew not the getting of: they think " It is day, and will never be night:" that a little to be spent out of so much is not worth minding; but always taking out of the meal-tub, and
never

never putting in, foon comes to the bottom," as Poor Richard fays; and then, "When the well is dry, they know the worth of water." But this they might have known before, if they had taken his advice. "If you would know the value of money, go and try to borrow fome; for he that goes a borrowing goes a forrowing," as Poor Richard fays; and, indeed, fo does he that lends to fuch people, when he goes to get in again. Poor Dick farther advifes, and fays,

"Fond pride of drefs is fure a very curfe;
Ere fancy you confult, confult your purfe."

And again, "Pride is as loud a beggar as Want, and a great deal more faucy." When you have bought one fine thing, you muſt buy ten more, that your appearance may be all of a piece; but Poor Dick fays, "It is eafier to fupprefs the firſt defire, than to fatisfy all that follow it:" And it is as truly folly
for

for the poor to ape the rich, as for the frog to swell, in order to equal the ox.

"Vessels large may venture more,
But little boats should keep near shore."

It is, however, a folly soon punished; for, as Poor Richard says, "Pride that dines on vanity, sups on contempt; Pride breakfasted with Plenty, dined with Poverty, and supped with Infamy." And, after all, of what use is this pride of appearance for which so much is risked, so much is suffered? It cannot promote health, nor ease pain; it makes no increase of merit in the person, it creates envy, it hastens misfortune.

"But what madness must it be to run in debt for these superfluities? We are offered, by the terms of this sale, six months credit; and that, perhaps, has induced some of us to attend it, because we cannot spare the ready money, and hope now to be fine without it. But, ah! think what you do when you run in debt; you give to another power

power over your liberty. If you cannot pay at the time, you will be afhamed to fee your creditor; you will be in fear when you fpeak to him; you will make poor pitiful fneaking excufes, and by degrees, come to lofe your veracity, and fink into bafe downright lying; for, " The fecond vice is lying, the firft is running in debt," as Poor Richard fays; and again, to the fame purpofe, " Lying rides upon Debt's back:" whereas a free American ought not to be afhamed, nor afraid to fee or fpeak to any man living. But poverty often deprives a man of all fpirit and virtue. " It is hard for an empty bag to ftand upright." What would you think of that nation, or of that government, who fhould iffue an edict, forbidding you to drefs like a gentleman or gentlewoman, on pain of imprifonment or fervitude? Would you not fay, that you were free, have a right to drefs as you pleafe, and that

that such an edict would be a breach of your privileges, and such a government tyrannical? And yet you are about to put yourself under that tyranny when you run in debt for such dress! Your creditor has authority, at his pleasure, to deprive you of your liberty, by confining you in gaol for life, or by selling you for a servant, if you should not be able to pay him: when you have got your bargain, you may perhaps think little of payment; but as Poor Richard says, " Creditors have better memories than debtors, creditors are a superstitious sect, great observers of set days and times." The day comes round before you are aware, and the demand is made before you are prepared to satisfy it; or, if you bear your debt in mind, the term, which at first seemed so long, will, as it lessens, appear extremely short: Time will seem to have added wings to his heels as well as his shoulders. " Those have

have a ſhort Lent, who owe money to be paid at Eaſter." At preſent, perhaps, you may think yourſelves in thriving circumſtances, and that you can bear a little extravagance without injury; but

"For age and want fave while you may,
No morning-ſun laſts a whole day."

GAIN may be temporary and uncertain, but ever, while you live, expence is conſtant and ..certain; and, " It is eaſier to build two chimneys, than to keep one in fuel," as Poor Richard ſays: So, " Rather go to bed ſupperleſs, than riſe in debt.

"Get what you can, and what you get hold,
'Tis the ſtone that will turn all your lead into gold."

AND when you have got the philoſopher's ſtone, ſure you will no longer complain of bad times, or the difficulty of paying taxes.

IV. " THIS doctrine, my friends, is reaſon and wiſdom: but, after all, do not depend too much upon your own
induſtry

industry and frugality, and prudence, though excellent things; for they may all be blasted, without the blessing of Heaven; and therefore, ask that blessing humbly, and be not uncharitable to those that at present seem to want it, but comfort and help them. Remember, Job suffered, and was afterwards prosperous.

" And now to conclude, " Experience keeps a dear school, but fools will learn in no other," as Poor Richard says, and scarce in that; for, it is true, " We may give advice, but we cannot give conduct:" However remember this, " They that will not be counselled cannot be helped;" and farther, that " If you will not hear Reason, she will surely rap your knuckles," as Poor Richard says.

Thus the old gentleman ended his harangue. The people heard it, and approved the doctrine, and immediately practised

practised the contrary, just as if it had been a common sermon; for the auction opened, and they began to buy extravagantly. I found the good man had thoroughly studied my Almanacks, and digested all I had dropt on those topics during the course of twenty-five years. The frequent mention he made of me must have tired any one else; but my vanity was wonderfully delighted with it, though I was conscious, that not a tenth part of the wisdom was my own, which he ascribed to me; but rather the gleanings that I had made of the sense of all ages and nations. However, I resolved to be the better for the echo of it; and, though I had at first determined to buy stuff for a new coat, I went away, resolved to wear my old one a little longer. Reader, if thou wilt do the same, thy profit will be as great as mine. I am, as ever, thine to serve thee.

RICHARD SAUNDERS.

ADVICE

TO A

YOUNG TRADESMAN.

Remember that *time* is money. He that can earn ten shillings a day by his labour, and goes abroad, or sits idle one half of that day, though he spends but sixpence during his diversion or idleness, ought not to reckon that the only expence; he has really spent, or rather thrown away, five shillings besides.

Remember that credit is money. If a man lets his money lie in my hands after it is due, he gives me the interest, or so much as I can make of it during that

that time. This amounts to a considerable sum when a man has good and large credit, and makes good use of it.

REMEMBER that money is of a prolific generating nature. Money can beget money, and its offspring can beget more, and so on. Five shillings turned is six; turned again, it is seven and three pence; and so on till it becomes an hundred pounds. The more there is of it, the more it produces, every turning, so that the profits rise quicker and quicker. He that kills a breeding sow, destroys all her offspring to the thousandth generation. He that murders a crown, destroys all that it might have produced, even scores of pounds.

REMEMBER that six pounds a year is but a groat a day. For this little sum, which may be daily wasted either in time or expence, unperceived, a man of credit may, on his own security, have the constant possession and use of an hundred

dred pounds. So much in stock, briskly turned by an industrious man, produces great advantage.

Remember this saying, " The good paymaster is lord of another man's purse." He that is known to pay punctually and exactly to the time he promises, may at any time, and on any occasion, raise all the money his friends can spare. This is sometimes of great use. After industry and frugality, nothing contributes more to the raising of a young man in the world, than punctuality and justice in all his dealings: therefore never keep borrowed money an hour beyond the time you promised, lest a disappointment shut up your friend's purse for ever.

The most trifling actions that affect a man's credit are to be regarded. The sound of your hammer at five in the morning, or nine at night, heard by a creditor, makes him easy six months longer;

longer; but if he sees you at a billiard table, or hears your voice at a tavern, when you should be at work, he sends for his money the next day; demands it before he can receive it in a lump.

It shews, besides, that you are mindful of what you owe; it makes you appear a careful, as well as honest man, and that still increases your credit.

Beware of thinking all your own that you possess, and of living accordingly. It is a mistake that many people who have credit fall into. To prevent this, keep an exact account, for some time, both of your expences and your income. If you take the pains at first to mention particulars, it will have this good effect; you will discover how wonderfully small trifling expences mount up to large sums, and will discern what might have been, and may for the future be saved, without occasioning any great inconvenience.

In

In short, the way to wealth, if you desire it, is as plain as the way to market. It depends chiefly on two words, *industry* and *frugality;* that is, waste neither *time* nor *money*, but make the best use of both. Without industry and frugality nothing will do, and with them every thing. He that gets all he can honestly, and saves all he gets, (necessary expences excepted) will certainly become *rich;* if that Being who governs the world, to whom all should look for a blessing on their honest endeavours, doth not, in his wise providence, otherwise determine.

AN OLD TRADESMAN.

PART III.

A

SURE GUIDE

TO

HAPPINESS,

BY

DOCTOR SCOTT.

A SURE GUIDE TO HAPPINESS.

> "Oh Happiness! our beings end and aim,
> "Good, pleasure, ease, content; whate'er thy name,
> "That something still which prompts th' eternal sigh,
> "For which we bear to live, or dare to die.
> "Plant of celestial seed, if dropt below,
> "Say in what favour'd soil thou deign'st to grow."
> POPE.

IF there be any truth fully ascertained by reason and revelation, it is this, That "*Man is not but to be happy.*" Surely the mighty author of our being can have no selfish view in our creation. His happiness is too immense and too secure to receive increase, or to suffer diminution from any thing that we can do. " *Can a man profit his Maker, or what need hath the Almighty of our services?*"

A MORE

A MORE important question claims our regard. Wherein *consists* the happiness of Man?

In order to answer this, we must remember, that man is composed of two natures, an animal and a rational, each of which is blest with capacities of enjoyment, and must have its correspondent objects of gratification before man can be happy. Hitherto we have considered him in the first of these, in his animal capacity: We have placed before us, *a creature of noble shape, erect and fair*, formed of nerves and fibres, and endued with appetites and feelings.

Though this his animal nature be infinitely inferior to his rational, yet since the happiness of the latter cannot be complete, while the former is destitute of its proper goods, we have devoted the two preceding books to the best interests of his animal nature. We have taken the liberty to send him to Old Cornaro

Cornaro and Dr. Franklin, to hear their excellent lectures on health and competence, which all allow to be two very choice ingredients in the cup of happinefs. Nay, fome entertain fo high an opinion of thefe, as to declare, that if Cornaro and Franklin could infufe a *quantum fufficit* of them, they would be content, and afk no better happinefs than what they could extract from thefe.

But let it be remembered that this is not the language of the wife, but of the flothful, and of fuch as are pufhed for money, who frequently experiencing the painfulnefs of being dunned, and fometimes tafting the fweets of eafe and pleafure, are ready to conclude, that if they had but money enough; Oh if they had but money enough to retire from the fatigues and vexations of bufinefs, and to fpend delicious days and nights in all the varied joys

joys of feasted sense, *how blest as the immortal Gods they would be!*

And truly, if man was but a more elegant sort of beast, and capable of no higher pleasures than those of sense, these Mahometan dreamers might be more than half in the right. In that case, health and competence might very well serve our turn; as with the one we might purchase, and with the other enjoy, all the happiness of which we were capable. But since God has been so good as to raise us many degrees above mere animal nature; since he has together with bodies, given us immortal minds, endowed with faculties and affections capable of angelic joys, it follows very delightfully, that another guess bill of fare must be made out for us, than that which would serve Epicurean hogs.

Those gentlemen who are so fond of stinting themselves to mere *bodily* pleasures, fures, would do well to remember, that every rank of animated nature muſt have its proper gratifications or be miferable. Furniſh earth and water to a *plant*, and it ſhall look green, and flouriſh like a cedar in Lebanon; but give nothing but this to a *horſe*, and he ſhall preſently periſh for want of nutriment. Again, give graſs and water to a horſe, and he ſhall look plump as pampered fpeculation; but confine a *man* to graſs and water, and you ſhall foon write *hic jacet* on his tomb. Thus every link in the great chain of being has its reſpective capacities and enjoyments. Man is favoured with theſe in a degree of perfection above all the creatures that we have feen. He poffeffes, harmoniouſly blended in himſelf, the various excellencies of two different natures; together with a reliſh for all the pleafures of the moſt perfect animal, he can boaſt capacities equal to the fublime delights of celestial spirits; now to suppose that so exalted, I had almost said so divine a creature as this, can be satisfied with enjoyments that belong to the poorest and meanest part of his nature, were a far greater absurdity, than to suppose that an animal of the most delicate taste and sense, can be content with earth and water, the simple nutriment of a plant.

ACCORDINGLY we find that experience has ever evinced the mistake of those, who have expected, that sensual goods *alone* could make them happy. This is not a novel opinion, but seems to have been a favourite notion of some in the days of King Solomon, who resolved to examine the truth or falsehood of it. Never man enjoyed equal opportunities; he had gold and silver as the stones in the vallies for abundance; and in wisdom he far exceeded all the sages of the East. The whole force of this wisdom and wealth he determined to employ on the experiment.

experiment. "*Behold* (said he) *I will get me down and make me great works, and build me houses, and plant me vineyards, and make me gardens and pools of water. I will get me men singers and women singers, and all the delights of the sons of men; and whatever mine eyes desire, I will not keep from them.*" When every thing is thus planned by himself, and executed according to his direction, surely he is arrived to the accomplishment of his wishes, and has ascended to the summit of all human happiness. The poor, who are taken with fine shows, would conclude so: Solomon certainly knows best; let us ask him, What does he say?

"*Lo! I looked on all the works that my hands had wrought, and on the labour that I had laboured to do, and behold all was vanity and vexation of spirit, and there was no profit under the sun.*" Well, gentlemen, you, I mean who think that
if

if you had but an abundance of *riches*, and *health* to *enjoy* them, you could not fail to be happy. What do you think of having againſt you ſuch a formidable caſe in point as this? Are you not beginning to ſuſpect that you may have been under a miſtake all this time? Suppreſs not the friendly ſuſpicion: Inſtead of repining, you ſhould rejoice to find that you have been in an error. Have you not abundant cauſe of joy, that riches and health with all their ſprings and ſtreams of pleaſure, are not *alone* ſufficient to quench your thirſt of happineſs, nor able to fill up the vaſt capacities of your nature? After conquering one world, Alexander ſat down and wept, that he had not another into which he could puſh his victories: But, thank God, we have not his cauſe of complaint.

For after having puſhed our conqueſts through all thoſe regions of innocent enjoyment

enjoyment which belong to our animal nature, we can enter upon the far wider provinces of REASON and AFFECTION, and poffefs ourfelves of all the fublime pleafures of angels, *i. e.* the pleafures of knowledge, imagination, virtue, friendfhip and love. When afked therefore, *Wherein confifts the true happinefs of Man?* We readily anfwer, that as the happinefs of a mere animal confifts in exercifing its appetites on fuch goods as are fuited to its nature, and capable of gratifying all its fenfes; fo the true happinefs of man confifts in exercifing his faculties on fuch objects as are fuited to his rational nature, and capable of delighting his foul through all her various affections. But where is that *infinite good?* Who is that wondrous being that can feaft the faculties, and fatisfy the defires of an *immortal mind?* 'Tis God; and he alone in whofe ineffable perfections the whole world of rationals

als will find enough, and more than enough, to employ their admiration and delight through eternal ages.

Accordingly we find that Christ, when asked what a man should do to be truly happy, replied, " *Thou shalt love the Lord thy God with all thy heart, and with all thy mind; and thou shalt love thy neighbour as thyself.*"

In this admirable reply, which for sublimity of piety and philanthropy, and for profound wisdom and philosophy, deserves everlasting veneration. We learn three very important lessons. I. That the chief good or true happiness of man consists in his mind. II. In the affections of his mind. And III. In those affections directed to worthy objects.

I. He who was perfectly acquainted with our nature, places the supreme happiness of man in the mind. How strange soever it may seem, yet most certain

certain it is, that this ever was, and still is a new doctrine to the bulk of mankind. For not only the numerous sect of ancient Epicureans, and sensual Mahometans, but the generality of Christians to this day, place the seat of happiness in the *body*.

TALK to them about the pleasures of the understanding, or the still sublimer pleasures of devotion, and your words seem not to be understood; but shift the subject, and talk about the pleasures of inheriting large estates, of living at ease and faring sumptuously every day, and immediately you perceive, by their smiling countenances and ready conversation, that you have awakened their favourite ideas, and that these are the things which lie nearest to their hearts.

THAT the goods of the body constitute some small part of man's happiness, and that therefore they ought to be valued, and, as far as conscience and
a regard

a regard to higher interests will permit, should be sought after, is *evident*. But that these goods and pleasures of the body, constitute man's *supreme* happiness, is one of the most degrading, damnable errors, that ever was broached. No man who understands the dignity of his immortal part, and who entertains a proper love for himself and his fellow men, can hear such a proposition without abhorrence and indignation. What! shall happiness which all so vehemently desire, and so heartily pray for, both for themselves and for others; shall happiness, the bare hope of which revives the heart, and does good like a medicine; which gives strength to the weak, and courage to the fearful; which animates us through life; nor deserts us in death—Shall this *fondest wish*, this *sweetest expectation* of all men, consist merely in the goods and pleasures of the body. Consider, thou cruel murderer

derer of thyfelf; thou barbarous affaffin of human kind, how few ever attain thofe pleafures to which thou ftupidly confineft the happinefs of man; how fewer ftill ever *enjoy* them, and how foon death will fnatch them out of the hands of thofe who are fo fortunate! Reflect what unnumbered millions are born to no better inheritance than poverty and bondage, and who, inftead of being careffed in the foft lap of eafe and pleafure, are driven through life by the fcourge of cruel tyrants, or more cruel wants! hard put to it to get a little bread, and fometimes *never* get *it*, at leaft not comfortably; but from various caufes, eat it all their lives long in bitternefs of foul! And of thofe feemingly happy ones who poffefs all the goods of the body, How few enjoy them without alloy? How many, by abufing thefe bleffings, contract difeafes which render fleeting life one con-

o tinued

tinued scene of sorrow and suffering? And in those apparently fortunate cases, where the greatest abundance of sensual goods is accompanied with health and power of enjoyment; yet, alas! how soon does enjoyment consume the little good which they contained, and leave the wealthy glutton to languish under indifference, to fret through disappointment, and to sigh for something else?

Cast your eyes on that pale bloated figure. It is the Emperor Heliogabalus, corrupted by the brutalizing sophistry of Epicurus, *i. e.* that the pleasures of the body constitute man's only happiness, he resolved to be happy to some purpose. All Italy was taxed; all Asia robbed to support his luxury; every region of the earth was explored; every element ransacked to furnish his table. All that bounteous nature bestows of rare and delicious among her birds, beasts, fishes, fruits and spices; and

all

all thefe prepared by the nicest hand of cookery, were ferved up to feaft and delight his appetites. Surely, if luxurious eafe and delicious fare were happinefs, Heliogabalus muft have been bleft indeed. The difcontent vifible in his countenance proves the reverfe. Could you afk him, he would tell you that his pleafures are at beft but vain, and too frequently vexatious. Sometimes he was mortified, becaufe, through defect of appetite, he could not enjoy his delicious morfels. At other times, tempted by their lufcious flavour, he fed to an excefs, which brought on him a variety of painful and loathfome difeafes. And at all times it was matter of grief to him, that the pleafures of eating and drinking fhould fo foon be over. This circumftance caufed one of the Roman Emperors to quarrel with his own conftitution, and to wifh, in all the rage of difappointed pleafure, that he had the

ftomach

stomach of a horse, that he might enjoy the satisfaction of eating ten times as much as its present scanty capacities would allow. And another Emperor, for the same swinish reason, preferred his petition to the Gods, that they would grant him a neck as long as that of a crane, vainly hoping, that he should thereby the longer enjoy the dear pleasure of swallowing.

But granting the sensuality an utter exemption from all the ills and vexations of gluttony; that his coveted dainties are all served up in the most inviting style of perfection; that his fruits are lusciously ripe and fresh; his meats tender and deliciously flavoured; his cookery the most exquisite in the world, and his wines equal to the nectar of Jove. And granting too that he has an appetite to season, and health to enjoy all these dainties, yet, alas! how soon must the season of enjoyment be

over

over with him forever! Old age will prefently fteal on him; his nerves muft foon grow hard and dull, and lofe their delicate edge and fenfibility, and then, though he may fit *down*, yet can he not enjoy his dainty morfels.

Behold, I am now (faid the rich old Barzillai) *fourfcore years old, and can I difcern what is favoury? Can I tafte what I eat or what I drink; or can I hear the voice of finging men and finging women?* After this humiliating period, what fad difhonours will ficknefs and death foon bring upon the body, the gluttons pampered pride! His cheeks once fo plump and rofy, are now pale and emaciated. His fkin, formerly fo fmooth and polifhed, is now deformed with wrinkles. His body once ftraight and erect, is now crooked and bent with years. His limbs, late fo nimble and active, are now ftiff and fcarcely able to move. And he who forty years ago poffeffed all the bloom and vigour of full formed manhood, is now shrunk away to mere skin and bone, and experiences all the helplessness of a second childhood.

Supported on his crutches or cane, he attempts to move, but it is with difficulty and pain. His knees knock against each other through weakness. His hands tremble, and his whole body shakes as with an ague. In a little time his infirmities prevail; his body, though but the shadow of his former self, is now too heavy for his exhausted strength. In a low faultering voice, he begs to be led to his bed, and there lies down never more to rise. Nature now sinks apace; his heart labours; his breast heaves; his breathing becomes short and quick; his eyes are hollow and sunk; his voice grows hoarse; he rattles in the throat; his limbs wax cold; his teeth turn black; he foams at the mouth; a feeble convulsion shakes his frame, and,

and, with a deep groan, his unwilling spirit takes her leave. Immediately putrefaction and worms begin their loathsome office; and in a little time, this pampered, idolized flesh, returns to the dust of which it was formed.

Who can contemplate this picture, and not bewail with tears of blood, the madness of those who expect their only happiness from such a *vile* body! O how infinitely superior to these miserable delusions is the Heaven descended philosophy of Jesus Christ! In that divine religion, the body, instead of being exalted as the seat of our happiness, is depreciated as the principal cause of our misery, being, as the poet expresses it, not only a nest of pain and bag of corruption, but the most fruitful source of our sins and sorrows. Christ seldom mentions the body, except to expose its comparative worthlessness, and to caution us against its defiling lusts. In
every

every part of the sacred volume, you hear his voice exclaiming with all the earnestness of parental affection: *" Woe be to him who trusteth in the body, and maketh flesh his hope, for wherein is it to be relied on? Its origin is but dust, its beauty but a flower, its life but a vapour, and its duration but a moment. Pain and weariness accompany it while living, corruption and worms seize on it when dead. O let not thine heart decline to its lusts, and yeild not to its enticements, for they have cast down many wounded; yea, many strong men have been slain by them; their way is the way to hell, going down by the chambers of death. But though in the body thou canst find no true content, yet think of thy soul and rejoice, for she is more precious than silver, yea much fine gold is not to be compared unto her. Her beginning is from the breath of the Almighty, and her duration is as the days of eternity. She was made but a little lower than the angels,*

angels, and heaven was prepared of old for the place of her habitation. Wouldst thou be happy, deck her with the jewels of piety, and cloath her with virtue as with a garment; then shall the lamp of the Almighty shine into thy heart, and joy shall be thy constant companion. When thou walkest by the way, thy foot shall not stumble; and when thou liest down, thy sleep shall be sweet. In the day of sickness thou shalt not be afraid, and when death cometh upon thee, thou shalt laugh him to scorn; for the Lord of hosts is thy friend, and underneath thee are the everlasting arms. He shall say unto thee, fear not, thou worm Jacob, for I am with thee; be not dismayed for I am thy God. Then shall he strip off thee the vile rags of mortality, and cloath thee with the garments of salvation. He shall wipe from thine eyes the tear of sorrow, and anoint thy face with the oil of gladness. He shall conduct thee into his own city, the city of the

the living God, and unto the general affembly of angels, and fpirits of juft men made perfect. He fhall give thee to drink with them of his rivers of pleafure, and to feaft on joys at his right hand forever more."

Thus fplendid are the honours and felicities of which the foul of man is capable. Thefe are the eternal goods to which Chrift intreats us to afpire, and for the fake of which, he bids us defpife the low unfatisfactory pleafures of a dying body.

What divine goodnefs, what perfect wifdom, are blended in that philofophy, which enjoins us to feek our happinefs in the *mind* and not in the *body*. In *that* part of our nature which exalts us to God, and not in that which depreffes us to the brute. In that part of us which will live forever, and not in that which is daily in danger of dropping into the grave. In that part of us which can enjoy the noble pleafures

fures of the glorious ones in Heaven, and not in that whofe few pleafures are in common with the creatures of the ftalls and ftyes.

But our divine Philofopher places the fupreme happinefs of man, not only in the mind, as we have juft feen, but

II. In the *affections* of the mind.

This alfo will appear to many as a ftrange faying. It muft expect to combat, not only the prejudices of coarfe Epicures, but the more ferious doubts of many who feem to be more refined and rational in their fchemes of happinefs. Many, even of thofe, who difdaining a vile body, funk their happinefs in the immortal mind, have never yet dreamed that it confifts in the affections, but have fought it rather in the improvements of the *underftanding*. Obferving the great refpect that is paid to men of learning, and remembering the high entertainment which they

they themselves have derived from the conversation of such men, they conclude, that learning must be the brightest ornament and highest happiness of human nature. In their estimation, the man whose comprehensive mind takes a wide survey of the works of God, and of the inventions of men; who soars into the Heavens, and calls the stars by name; calculates eclipses, and foretells comets; who thence goes down into the depths of the sea, and explains the causes of its ceaseless motions; who traverses the boundless regions of the earth, knows *all their kingdoms, with the glory of them;* who speaks various languages, fathoms the depths of arts and sciences, understands the history of nations, the laws and government of all people. This, in their estimation, is the truly happy man. In a mind thus richly furnished, he possesses (as they suppose) the materials of an an enjoyment, of which nothing can ever deprive him.

Far be it from me to speak disrespectfully of learning, for certainly learning or wisdom is the *pia mater*, or first attribute of God himself, and the vast circumference within which lies all the happiness that human or angelic minds can enjoy. But this I say, that all the learning in the world, if separated from the *affections*, can never make us truly happy: And that these splendid attainments in science were never intended to form the *supreme* happiness of man, is evident, because the bulk of mankind are not capable of becoming great scholars and philosophers. Alas! What numbers, after all the pains that have been taken with them, never learn even to read their mother tongue with propriety! How many, who after a seven years apprenticeship, and a whole life's employment, never learn to fit on a handsome

handsome boot or shoe! Many born with genius equal to the attainment of learning, are constrained to live and die in ignorance, for want of means to defray the expence of education; while others are obliged to stop in the middle of their career, and to give up the fond hopes of knowledge, because of a constitution too delicate to bear the fatigues of study. But granting to the lover of learning, every advantage of genius, constitution and fortune, that ever fell to the lot of the most favoured of mankind, what mighty acquisitions can be made by him whose genius is, at best, but dulness, and whose days are but a moment! When he considers the secrets of art, so multiplied and mysterious, he sits down in despair. When he contemplates the works of God, so infinite and unsearchable, the spirit faints within him, and he seems to himself, but as a feather floating on the surface of of a mighty ocean, whofe wonders he can never explore. And were he afked for the fum of his learning, he would, if honeft, take up the lamentation of the old philofopher, and reply, that after the vain toils of threefcore years, he has learned to know that he knows nothing.

But admitting that he has acquired that ftock of learning on which vain mortals are fo adventurous as to fet up for *mafters* and *doctors*. Admitting that he has learned languages, ftudied arts and fciences, &c. &c. What is there in all this to make him happy, or to fatisfy the defires of an immortal mind? As to languages, what folly to dream as fome do, of great wifdom and honour to be found in learning them! For, What is language but words or founds by which we communicate our thoughts to one another? If thefe words or founds had the power like

charms,

charms, to brighten our wits, or to better our hearts, this language-mongery would be a noble speculation; but, alas! instead of making us wiser, these *learned* languages often make us greater fools. For, allowing, that after an expence of five years, and of at least as many hundred pounds, a young man has learned enough to give his horse a Latin or Greek name; What mighty advantages does he derive from this pretty art of nick-naming God's creatures? Does it teach him any new ideas relative to the nature and qualities of a horse? Or can it furnish him one useful receipt in farriery, or a single rule for the better management and choice of that noble animal?

Evidently, therefore, the *summum bonum*, or chief good of man does not consist in *dead languages*.

And as to systems of human learning, from which some fondly expect unfailing

ing pleasure and eternal honour, what are they, *frequently*, but systems of human error, monuments of the pride of man, who, impatient to be thought ignorant of any thing, boldly seizes fancy for fact, and conjecture for evidence, and with these fairy workmen, presently runs up vast Babels of *philosophy, vainly so called.* A whole lifetime is hardly sufficient to understand these pompous errors; and scarcely are they understood, before they are exploded to make room for some other set of notions, equally vain and perishable.

But, admitting that we have turned our studies to the noblest of human sciences, sciences founded on truth, and promising much entertainment and useful knowledge; yet, alas! full soon shall experience prove the truth of the remark made by Solomon, that " *In much learning is much trouble ; and he who increases knowledge, increases sorrow.*" See! how

how *enviously,* sharp thorns and briars shoot up among the sweet flowers which we expected to gather. To make any considerable progress in sciences, we must renounce some of the freedom and amusements of life; this is mortifying; confinement is wearisome; hard study fatigues the brain; intense thinking sours the temper; slow progress is disheartening; doubts are vexatious; and presently darkness and thick clouds gather over the path of science, and forbid us to proceed any farther. *Surely man walketh in a vain shadow, and disquieteth himself in vain.*

But supposing that we could understand all human sciences in the most perfect degree, how very short lived would be the pleasures arising from them! When first made, and fresh on the mind, the discoveries of truth are highly gratifying to curiosity, but in a short time they become familiar, and thence

thence almoſt inſipid. Hence we often ſee learned men as diſcontented and peeviſh as others; a plain proof that *human learning* opens no ſpring of laſting happineſs in the mind. Indeed, ſo far from producing this very deſireable effect, it frequently nurſes paſſions the moſt *unfriendly* to his happineſs, both in this world and the next. The brighter talents and ſuperior fame of a rival wit, often pierce his heart with the keeneſt pangs of envy; ſucceſs puffs him up with pride, and renders him inſufferably diſagreeable; diſappointment fires him with rage, or ſinks him into deſpondency: While the flaſh of an unguarded witticiſm often loſes him a valuable friend, or creates a mortal enemy. But allowing that he were the greateſt ſcholar and orator of the age, and could harangue on any ſubject, with all the force of argument and charms of eloquence: that whenever he appeared ed, the impatient crowds repaired to hear the magic of his enchanting tongue: that princes were his patrons, and the great ones of the earth his admirers; yet how vain and treacherous a good would all this be! How utterly unworthy to be coveted as the chief good of man! For yet but a few fleeting years, and the cold hand of age will be on him, and then, alas! all thefe fine talents and blooming honours, fhall perifh as the lovely flower perifhes when touched by the killing frofts of winter. His wit fhall fparkle no more; no more fhall his fancy charm us with the fplendor of its images, nor his mind aftonifh us with the vaftnefs of her conceptions; his memory muft then give up all her precious treafures; and dumb forever will be that tongue whofe eloquence, like fweeteft mufic, foothed each liftening ear, and led in triumph all the obedient paffions.

AND

And are such fading accomplishments as these, fit food for an immortal soul that was born for heaven?

But although this acknowledged vanity and vexation of human learning, sufficiently proves the sad mistake of those who make an *idol* of it; yet let us not, on the other hand, run into the equal error of such as trample it under their feet as vain and worthless altogether. Along with its dross, it contains much useful metal, for the sake of which we may well afford to toil.

Even the *languages*, though the *least* necessary of all human learning, are not entirely without their uses. We may chance to fall in with a poor foreigner, who has not broken English enough to tell us his wants. We may get honest bread by interpreting, translating, or teaching languages. Or should it be our fortune to stand behind a counter,

ter, we may, with the help of a little *bad* French, sell a great deal of *good* merchandize. We may likewise find much *pleasure* in reading the enchanting works of foreign poets, historians, &c. and this effect may lead to one still more valuable; it may inspire us with sentiments of friendship for the nation to which these excellent men belong, and thus happily moderate that resentment, which, under certain circumstances we might feel against them. These effects, in a very comfortable degree, I have myself experienced. I have found, that my passions, kindling into pain from the blows struck our unoffending country, by the British, have been considerably calmed by recollecting, that these our *injurers*, are the children of the same once *glorious island* which gave to us and to all mankind, a Milton, a Newton, a Locke, a Barrow, and other UNEQUALLED LIGHTS

of

of philosophy and divinity, whose friendly splendors have contributed so happily to repel the coming clouds of "*chaos and old night,*" and to establish the empire of reason and *pure* religion.

HITHERTO we have endeavoured to point out the mistake of those, (a numerous race) who look for happiness among sensual pleasures, and in human learning. Two other orders of candidates, equally numerous, and, as I think, equally mistaken, present themselves,—I mean the hardy sons of avarice and ambition. The first of these, the miser, blesses God; wonders how people can be so weak as to throw away their time and money on *book learning* and *silly pleasures.* He has juster notions of things. Gold is with him *the one thing needful. He rises early, early, late takes rest, and eats the bread of carefulness and toil, in order to join house to house,*

and

and field to field, and thus to remove himself far from all dread of want.

But of wealth it may be said, *happiness is not here*. Gold, it is true, is the quintessence of lands, houses, soft cloathing, sumptuous fare, and of every other pleasure that flesh and blood is heir to. But evident it is to *reason*, that all the treasures on earth can never satisfy an immortal soul: And Scripture asserts, that: "*A man's life consisteth not in the abundance of the things which he possesseth.*" And whose experience doth not witness it? We call the rich *happy!* Alas! could we but see their anxious cares, their inward restlessness, the miseries of desires delayed or disappointed, which sometimes attend even the most fortunate; could we know their constant fears of losing, and their thirst for more, which suffers them not to enjoy their present gains; could we follow one who is "*making haste to be rich*," through all

all his toils and labours, his weary days and sleepless nights, and all his various vexations, we should be fully convinced of the truth of this, that *he who increaseth riches, increaseth sorrow.*

I MAY appeal to every man's heart who has sought happiness from this quarter, if this has not been his constant experience. You promised yourself that you should be perfectly happy when the other thousand was added to your stock, or the next purchase enlarged you estate: You had your wish, and yet you still wanted: Something was lacking. You proposed new additions, and waited for your happiness again; but a new thirst urged you again to new cares and to new toils. And if the time should ever come, that you shall think that you have enough, and like the rich man in the gospel, " *begin to pull down your barns and build greater; and to say to your soul, Soul, thou hast much goods*

goods laid up for many years, take thine ease, eat, drink, and be merry:" Then expect the final disappointment in that alarming message, " *Thou fool, this night shall thy soul be required of thee; then whose shall all those things be which thou hast so laboriously laid up?*"—Such is the happiness of those who *trust in uncertain riches.*

The ambitious seeks his happiness in the attainment of honour: And indeed to be distinguished in the world, treated with respect, spoken of with admiration, caressed and courted by all around us, is highly pleasing to the heart of man, and, in the eyes of many, possesses charms far superior to the vanities of pleasure, or the sordidness of gain; yet doth the desire of wordly esteem remove the soul as far from true happiness as the former. The enjoyment arising from the honour which cometh from man, stand continually on a precarious

carious foundation; it totters before every blast of disrespect, and every rumour of malevolence. *Like grass on the house top, it often withereth before it is plucked up;* For what can stand before envy? The hopes of men, like bubbles in the air, usually burst as they expand. The labours of ambition are disappointed, the pride of honor mortified, the idol of reputation broken to pieces, and the friendships of the world generally faithless.

Alas! That man, born for heaven, should waste his short day of grace in torturing himself to conform to the humours of a vain world; seeking a phantom of fame lighter than air; grasping at distinctions vain and insignificant; staking his happiness on the beck or breath of worms like himself; and after all, too frequently obliged to take up the lamentation of the once great Cardinal Woolsey: " *Had I but served God as faithfully as I have served the world, he would not thus have forsaken me in my grey hairs."*

But the vanity of seeking happiness from riches, honors and pleasures, is yet more convincingly felt when death comes to put a final close to this mortal scene. Ah! my friends, this is the awful hour that strips off the tinsel coverings of folly, stamps vanity on all beneath the sun, and shews that

"Too low they build, who build beneath the stars."

In that day of terror and despair, what can a vain world offer its poor deluded followers? Will a party of pleasure suit the chamber of sickness? Or the songs of folly delight the ear that listens with trembling to the striking hour? What music will sound in concert with dying groans? Or what joy can jewels and brocades afford when the shroud is ready to supplant them? Will the sparkling bowl revive any longer, when the parched

ched tongue begins to faulter? Or beauty kindle the *unhallowed fire* when death fits on the fixed eye balls, and spreads his chilling damps over the heart? Alas! my brother, *vanity of vanities, all is vanity,* is now seen in characters too legible to be overlooked. The remembrance of a life mispent in *vain* or in guilty pleasures, will fill the soul with pangs of remorse, with agonies of horror, of which none but the wretched sufferers can form any idea. *" Ah pleasure, pleasure, Thou vile sorceress! Thou cursed destroyer of my soul! Thou once smiledst as with the charms of innocence, now I feel thee sting as a viper. Where are thy promises of delight? Fool that I was to believe thee! For thy sake I have enslaved my soul to the lusts of a brute, and cherished the passions of a demon! I have neglected God, and sold my birth-right to heaven! Me. miserable! Whether am I going? My golden sands are all run out! The sun*

sun of my life is about to set, and, utterly unprepared, I am going to appear before God. Oh! that I had but my precious days to go over again! Eternal God, if thy mercy be infinite, exert it now to save such a self-ruined wretch as I am!"

But will *riches* better stand the test of that day's trial? Alas! they who have *put their confidence in fine gold, will find that it profits not in the day of wrath.* When death lifts his arm, and swift as lightening, disease and pain enter the heart, vain is the hoarded treasure. See that generally esteemed happy man who trusted in riches, stretched upon the bed of languishing; his body is panting for breath; his throat is parched; his heart flutters; his eyes grow dim; and life's silver cord is loosing: What joy now can riches bring? Surround his dying bed with bags of gold, will they alleviate the pains of the body, purchase a moment's respite from death, or silence the

the agonizing remonftrances of confcience? Alas! a golden God is but a dumb idol, neither *able to kill nor make alive.*

THEN, when earth, and only earth, hath been the purfuit, what wretchednefs to be torn from all that was counted happinefs; to leave this dear world behind them forever, to go——Ah! Whither? Not to *treafures laid up for them in heaven;* not to the place *where they have made themfelves friends of the mammon of unrighteoufnefs;* but where that *rich* man went who *lift up his eyes in torment, becaufe, though rich in this world, he was not rich towards God.*

Now, this is the boafted happinefs of numbers. This is the unutterable pleafure of dying worth fo many thoufand pounds.

"Guilt's blunder, and the loudeft laugh of hell."

YOUNG.

Nor

Nor will HONOR and FAME render our departure at all more comfortable.

SEND forth your imagination to view the laſt ſcene of the greateſt and proudeſt man who ever awed and governed the world. See a poor, infirm, miſerable, ſhort-lived creature, that paſſes away like a ſhadow, and is haſtening off the ſtage where the theatrical titles and diſtinctions, and the whole maſk of pride which he has worn for a day, will fall off and leave him naked as a neglected ſlave. Behold the empty vapour diſappearing! One of the arrows of mortality this moment ſticks faſt within him: See, it forces out his life, and freezes his blood and ſpirits.

APPROACH *his bed of ſtate,*—draw aſide the curtain,—regard a moment with ſilence.

ARE theſe cold hands and pale lips all that are left of him who was canonized

ized by his own pride, or made a god of by his flatterers?

O God! What is man? Even a thing of nought.

Alas! That a being whose existence on earth is but for a moment, and whose future mansion is heaven; a being whose immortal soul carries its hopes far beyond time, and extends them even to eternity, should set his mind on objects which time destroys! What is this but to mistake the changeable colours of the dew-drop for the lustre of the ruby, or the radiance of the diamond?

" *Lay not up for yourselves treasures on earth,*" says the divine Teacher. Long tossed by tumultuous passions, enraptured and alarmed with hopes and fears, we at last find *earth's* boasted treasures to be vain; its riches, honors, and pleasures utterly insufficient to make us happy. Full seldom are they obtained by the anxious candidate, and seldomer still

still without much pain and labour; and after all, made tastelefs by disease or age, or embittered by vexation, they are held but a few feverish years, and then forgotten forever in the grave.

"*Lay not up for yourselves treasures on earth, where moth and rust do corrupt, and where thieves break through and steal; but lay up for yourselves treasures in heaven; for where the treasure is, there will the heart be also.*"——What treasures? Why love,—Love to God and to our neighbour.

These are the true treasures; the treasures of the heart. No pleasures are comparable to those that affect the heart; and there are none that affect it with such exquisite delight, as loving and being beloved by a worthy object. Ask the young Theodosius, and he will tell you, that the most delicious feelings his heart ever experienced, were those of virtuous love; and that he never knew

knew what rapture was until he saw the incomparable Constantia, in whose person and manners are concentered all the charms of beauty, and all the graces of virtue.

Now, if love, when directed to a creature, can open such a heaven in our bosoms, what must it do when directed to God, the eternal fountain of all perfection and goodness? Would you know the blessing of all blessings, it is this *love* dwelling in the soul, sweetening our bitter, lightening our dark, enlivening our sad, and filling to the full of joy the souls that must ever thirst until they come to this great fountain of all happiness. There is no peace, nor ever can be for the soul of man, but in the exercise of this love; for as love is the infinite happiness that created man; so love is the only perfection and felicity of man; and no one can live in happiness, but as he lives in love. Look at

every

every pain and diforder in human nature, you will find it to be nothing elfe but the fpirit of the creature turned from love to felfifhnefs; and thence, in courfe, to anxiety, fear, covetoufnefs, wrath, envy, and all evil: So that love alone is, and only can be, the cure of every evil; and he who lives in love is rifen out of the power of evil into the freedom and joy of one of the fpirits of heaven. All wants are fatisfied, all diforders of nature are removed; no life is any longer a burden; every day is a day of peace; every thing is a fpring of joy to him who breathes the fweet gentle element of love.

But fome men, of gloomy and melancholic humours, will afk, Is it certain that God loves mankind? Surely the innumerable favours which he lavifhes upon us, muft fet his love beyond all doubt.

To

To afk whether God loves mankind, is indeed to afk whether he is good, which is the fame as queftioning his very exiftence; for how is it poffible to conceive a God without goodnefs? And, what goodnefs could he have were he to hate his own works, and to defire the mifery of his creatures?

A good prince loves his fubjects; a good father loves his children: We love even the tree we have planted; the houfe we have built; and is it poffible for God not to love mankind? Where can fuch a fufpicion rife, except in the minds of thofe who form a capricious and barbarous being of God; a being who makes a cruel fport of the fate of mankind; a being who deftines them, before they are born, to hell, referving to himfelf one, at moft, in a million, and that one no more meriting that preference, than the others have deferved their damnation? Impious blaf-
phemers,

phemers, who endeavour to give me an averſion to God, by perſuading me that I am the object of *his* averſion!

You will ſay, he owes nothing to man; well, but he owes ſomething to *himſelf;* he muſt neceſſarily be *juſt* and *beneficent.* If a virtuous heathen could declare that he had much rather it ſhould never be ſaid that there was ſuch a man as Plutarch, than that he was cruel and revengeful, how muſt the *Father* of *mercies* be diſpleaſed to find himſelf charged with ſuch hateful qualities?

Besides, I know he loves me, by the very love I feel for him; it is becauſe he loves me that he has engraved on my heart this ſentiment, the moſt precious of all his gifts. His love is the ſource of mine, as it ought to be, indeed, a motive to it.

Give me leave, in order to convey an idea of the love of God, to deſcribe the paſſion of a virtuous lover for his miſtreſs

miſtreſs. The compariſon in itſelf has nothing indecent. Love is a vice only in vicious hearts. Fire, though the pureſt of all ſubſtances, will yet emit unwholeſome and noxious vapours when it is fed by tainted matter; ſo love, if it grow in a vicious mind, produces nothing but ſhameful deſires and criminal deſigns, and is followed with fear, vexation and miſery. But let it riſe in an upright heart, and be kindled by an object adorned with virtue as well as beauty, it is ſafe from cenſure; far from being offended, God gives it his approbation. He has made amiable objects only that they might be loved.

Now let us ſee what paſſes in the heart of a perſon deeply ſmitten with love. He thinks with delight of the perſon beloved; he hurries with impetuoſity towards the charming object, and whatever keeps or removes him from her is tormenting; he is afraid of giving her any displeasure; he inquires into her taste and inclinations, in order to comply with and gratify them; he likes to hear her commended; talks of her with satisfaction, and caresses every thing that renews the agreeable idea.

It is a mistake to think that there is an essential difference between this and divine love. We have but one way of loving: Men love God and their friends in the same manner; and these affections differ only in the diversity of their objects and ends. Thus a pious man filled with sentiments towards God, like those of a virtuous lover, would be glad to behold him, and to be united to him; he thinks of him with delight, and speaks of him with reverence; he rejoices to see him honored, and is happy to hear him praised; he meditates on his laws with pleasure, and obeys them with alacrity.

That

That this love by which a pious mind is united to its Creator, is a source of the purest pleasures, we now proceed to shew, not solely on the authorities of scripture, but by the force of reason and common sense.

The man who loves God, enjoys that first of felicities, the *consciousness* of having placed his affections on the only object in the universe that truly deserves them. Our love is the most precious thing we possess; it is indeed the only thing we can properly call our own, and therefore to bestow it unworthily, is the greatest shame and sorest mistake that we can ever commit. A man must needs be infinitely mortified and troubled, when he finds that the object of his love possesses not that excellence which he fondly expected would satisfy his wishes and make him completely happy. Alas! What is a little skin deep beauty, a few flashes of wit, or some

some small degrees of goodness? We soon see to the bottom of such shallow goods, and consequently must experience a decay of that admiration and affection which constitutes happiness in the first degree. But to no such mortifying disappointment is he liable, who directs his love to God. In him the enlightened eye of true philosophy discovers so much of all that is great and good, as to keep the happy mind in an eternal extacy of admiration and love.

DIVINE love advances the happiness of man, because it tends, above all other attachments, to refine and ennoble his nature. The most inattentive must have observed, that love has a surprizing force to give our manners a resemblance to those of the person we love. Seen through the eyes of a tender affection, even blemishes appear like beauties, and heaven born virtue puts on charms more than human. No wonder then that we so easily adopt the sentiments, and imitate the manners of those we love. This is a conduct so natural and common, that to tell the character of any man, we need but be told that of the person he loves.

Hence, the anxious parent rejoices to see his child fond of the society of the virtuous and wise: he knows that such an attachment indicates a relish for virtue, and promises an honourable and happy event: while, on the other hand, he deplores his attachment to the vain and vicious, as a sad, but certain presage of folly and depravity.

Certainly then, in order to be happy, it most nearly concerns us to direct our love to the proper object. But who, or what is that object? The creatures all have their imperfections. They are all utterly unworthy, and beneath the supreme love of an immortal mind. And to love these in the extreme, is
infinitely

infinitely to demean ourselves, to disgrace our understandings, to contract low earthly passions, and consequently to make ourselves miserable. Would we do honour to our reason, would we dignify our affections, ennoble our nature, and rise to true happiness, let us give our hearts to God. The man who loves God is animated with an ambition becoming the dignity of his birth; he is inspired with a greatness of soul that spurns all grovelling passions and base designs. The love which he has for God impells him, by a sweet and powerful influence, to imitate his all lovely and adorable perfections, and consequently renders him every day a more divine and heavenly creature.

God is the only worthy object of our love, because he is the only one who will certainly and generously reward it. Love, as we have observed, was designed to be the spring of joy, but, alas! when

when placed on the creature, it often proves a source of sorrow, because it is too often treated with ingratitude and neglect. The lover in giving his heart, gives his *all;* and, if after so great a sacrifice, he cannot obtain the fond return he coveted, what can be expected but that he should sicken with grief, and sink under an oppressive load of melancholy? But though our fellow worms should reject our love with disdain, yet it is always—O! adorable goodness! it is always acceptable to God. Amidst the adorations of millions of glorious angels, he graciously observes the attentions we pay him, and receives with complacency our smallest tribute of affection. He knows that the souls which he has made cannot be happy until they return to him. Unceasingly he calls to them—

" SEEK ye my face." And if, convinced by a thousand disappointments, of the vanity of all other loves, we should at length, happily take up our resolution and say, *"Thy face, O God, we will seek."* Immediately his preventing love meets us more than half way; the harps of Heaven swell with louder strains of joy, and songs of congratulation fill the eternal regions.

DIVINE love infinitely exceeds in point of true happiness, all other attachments, because, it does not, like them, expose us to the pangs of separation. If that sweet passion, which, with chains dearer than those of gold, unites earthly lovers, were never to be dissolved, it would be well: But, alas! this is a felicity which Heaven has not thought fit to confer on erring mortals. The iron hand of necessity or duty often tears us away from our dearest friends, and consigns us to wearisome months of mutual fears and restless longings for re-union. Sometimes, in the happiest moments

moments of friendſhip, the thought of death occurs and throws a ſudden damp on our riſing joys. Sometimes it is our lot to ſit by the ſick beds of thoſe we love, and hear their piercing moans, to mark, with unutterable anguiſh, the faultering ſpeech and ſinking eye, or wipe the cold damps of death from thoſe cheeks which we have kiſſed a thouſand times. Such ſcenes and ſeparations, and all mortal loves are liable to ſuch, occaſion a grief not to be equalled by all the misfortunes of life, and make us dearly pay for all the paſt pleaſures of friendſhip.

IN theſe melancholy moments we are made to feel how truly bleſſed are they who have made the eternal God their love, nothing can ever ſeparate them from him. When the faireſt of the human fair are gone down into the duſt, and have left their lovers to mourning and woe. Nay, when after millions of revolving years, the sun is extinguished in the skies, and the lamps of heaven have lost their golden flames; when old time himself is worn away, and nature sunk under the weight of years; even then the God Jehovah will be the same, and his days shall never fail. Even then shall his triumphant lovers behold his glorious face cloathed in eternal beauty, and shall drink of the rivers of pleasure that flow at his right-hand forevermore. Neither will the lovers of God ever experience, even in this world, the pangs of separation from him, while they walk firmly in the golden path of duty. Should they be driven from their homes, and obliged to forsake their dearest friends; should they be compelled to plough distant seas, or to toil in the remotest regions of the earth; even there they will sweetly feel that

"They cannot go where universal love reigns not
"around." THOMPSON.

Even

Even there they meet and rejoice in their ever prefent friend; with facred pleafure they inhale his breath in the fragrant gale, they mark his pencil adorning the fields and meadows in their flowery pride; or with fublimeft awe, they behold his hand fwelling the everlafting mountains, or,

"Hanging the vaft expanfe in azure bright, and cloath-
"ing the fun in gold."

YOUNG.

HENCE it is, that the man who loves God is feldom lonefome, feldom knows what it is to want agreeable company. A great addition this to our happinefs! For as man is by nature a focial being, he muft be miferable unlefs he has fome beloved friend to converfe with. But, as thofe who do not love God, take little or no delight in converfing with him, they become more dependent on the company and converfation of their earthly friends. And, when deftitute

of

of thefe, they are often found, though in palaces, to be reftlefs and wretched.

Oh! how difconfolate is the condition of the man, who, though always prefent with his maker, yet finds no joy nor fatisfaction in his prefence! Though every particle of matter is actuated by this almighty being; though nature, through all her works, proclaims his wifdom, power, and goodnefs, unutterable; yet the man who is a ftranger to divine love, views all this wonderful fcenery

"With a brute unconfcious gaze."——Thompson.

He taftes none of that facred joy which thefe things were meant to infpire. The divinity is with him and in him, and every where about him, but is of no advantage to him. It is in fact the fame thing to him as if there were no God in the world.

Happily different is the condition of the man who loves the great author of his

his being! When that divine paſſion, (the ſoul's true light) is ſet up in our hearts, the ſcales of blindneſs fall from our eyes, the ſhades of night fly far away, and God, the bleſſed God, ſtands confeſſed before our admiring view. Tho' we cannot behold him with the eyes of ſenſe, yet, we can feel his preſence, we can *taſte and ſee* his adorable perfections which ſhine ſo brightly on all his glorious works.

WHEN we conſider the infinite hoſt of ſtars which adorn the evening ſkies; when, enlarging the idea, we contemplate another heaven of ſuns and worlds riſing ſtill higher, and theſe again enlightened by a ſtill ſuperior firmament of luminaries, overwhelmed by ſuch an immenſity of proſpect, we ſcarcely breathe out—" *Eternal God! what is man that thou art mindful of him, or the Son of Man that thou regardeſt him!*"

WHEN,

When, leaving these amazing scenes, we contemplate other parts of the divine dominions; when we walk through the fields and observe his wondrous workmanship in the touring trees or humbler shrubs; in the gentle rill or majestic flood; in the birds winging their airy flight, or perched on branches warbling their melodious lays; in the peaceful flocks grazing their simple pastures with herds of nobler cattle; or, in the swarms of gilded insects that, with ceaseless buzz, and vigorous motion, present their golden wings to the sun. In these, in all his infinitely varied creatures, we see, we admire, we adore the great creator.

The man whom love has thus taught to correspond with God, enjoys the most delightful and improving society. In the deepest solitude where others are depressed, he is happy, because he knows that he is with the greatest and best of beings;

beings: and when his earthly friends have withdrawn their agreeable company, he returns with still superior pleasure to that of his heavenly.

Divine love adds greatly to our happiness, because it disposes us to rejoice in every thing that seems connected with the honor of God. His Sabbath, his house, &c. become objects of our most hearty love and delight.

We live in a country, where one day in every week is set apart for the public worship of God. To the man who loves not his maker, this disposition of the seventh day is not very likely to be pleasing. As he is not a religious man, it is more than probable that he is a man of the world, a man of business or pleasure; and in either case the Sabbath must be unwelcome, as it is an interruption, and indeed a clear loss of one day's pleasure or profit in every week. A loss, which in the course of years must grow to be very

very serious: For, if we take fifty, (the number of tastelefs and unprofitable Sabbaths in the year,) and multiply those by seventy, (the years in a veteran's life) we shall find that it will amount to eight or ten years. Now, out of so short a life as threescore and ten, to be obliged to spend eight or ten years in lounging, moping, tiresome Sabbaths, must appear to men who have their interests and pleasures at heart, a heavy tax, a great drawback. Surely such men would give their thanks; nay, I suppose, would chearfully vote the thanks of all christendom to him, who should put them in the way to make the Sabbath the most agreeable day in the week. Let us love God, and the work is done. We shall then rejoice that there is such a day, because our hearts will then approve the purposes for which it was appointed. A day that is taken from the cares of a short life,

life, and laid out on the interests of eternity. A day that is spent in considering our obligations to God, in thanking him for his favours, confessing our unworthiness, and imploring his forgiveness; in short, a day spent in a way so admirably adapted to instruct the ignorant, to reclaim the bad, to strengthen the good, to honour God, and to make ourselves happy; such a day must, to him who loves God and man, be the most joyful day of the whole week.

On this account too, the man who loves God, will see a church in quite another light, and with sentiments happily different from those of the man who loves him not. To the latter, prayers, psalms and sermons, have always been wearisome; and, as it is in the church that he has been accustomed to do such penance, he insensibly contracts a dislike to it, and comes at last

laſt to view it with ſentiments ſuch as thoſe with which an idle boy regards his ſchool-houſe.

But the pious man, conſidering the church as the place where people meet to honor the God whom he *delights* to honor, to learn and love that goodneſs which he ſees to be ſo eſſential to the happineſs of the world, ſuch a man regards the church as the moſt beautiful and lovely building in the world; and the view of it gives him a more ſincere pleaſure than that which others feel in viewing the places of their moſt favourite amuſement.

" How amiable are thy tabernacles, O God of hoſts; how pleaſant is the place where thine honor dwelleth!"

But if gratitude, when exerted from man to man, produces ſo much pleaſure, it muſt exalt the ſoul to rapture, when it is employed on this great object of gratitude, on this infinitely beneficent

cent being, who has given us every thing we already poffefs, and from whom we expect every thing we yet hope for. When a good man looks around him on this vaft world, where beauty and goodnefs are reflected from every object, and where he beholds millions of creatures in their different ranks, enjoying the bleffings of exiftence, he looks up to the *univerfal Father*, and his heart glows within him. And in every comfort which fweetens his *own* life, he difcerns the fame indulgent hand. Is he bleft with tender parents, or with generous friends who prefs him with their kindnefs? Is he happy in his family rifing around him, in the wife who loves him, or in the children who give him comfort and joy? In all thefe pleafing enjoyments, in all thefe beloved objects he recognizes the hand of God. Every fmile of love, every act of tendernefs is an effect of
his

his goodnefs. By him was kindled every fpark of friendfhip that ever glowed on earth, and therefore to him it juftly returns laden with the pureft incenfe of gratitude. Has God prepared a table for him, and caufed his cup to overflow? Inftead of afcribing it to the policy of his own councils, or to the ftrength of his own arm, he gives the praife to him alone, who ftrews the earth with good things for man, and teaches him wifdom to improve and convert them to his own ufe.

THUS it is that gratitude prepares a good man for the enjoyment of profperity; for not only has he as full a relifh as others of the innocent pleafures of life, but, moreover, in thefe he holds communion with God. In all that is good or fair, he traces *his* hand. From the beauties of nature, from the improvements of art, from the bleffings of public or private life, he raifes his affections to the great

great fountain of all the happiness which surrounds him, and thus widens the sphere of his enjoyments, by adding to the pleasures of sense, the far more exquisite joys of the heart.

But divine love adds greatly to our happiness, not only by giving a fresh flavour to the sweets of prosperity; but by correcting in an eminent degree, the bitterness of *adversity*.

As in times of prosperity, among perhaps a few real friends, many pretended ones intrude themselves, who in the hour of distress are quickly dispersed and know us no more; so in those times also, many false and pretended joys court the affections and gain the heart of inconsiderate man. But, when calamity comes, those vain *joys* immediately discover their deceitful nature, desert the astonished man in his greatest need, and leave him a prey to shame, sorrow and remorse.

Adversity is the grand test of what is true and what is false among the different objects of our choice; and our love of God, tried by this test will soon discover its infinite value and excellence. Persons of every character are liable to distress. The man who loveth God, and he who loveth him not, is exposed to the stroke of adversity. But on the bad man, adversity falls with double weight, because it finds them without defence and without resource. When his health, his riches and pleasures, in which he placed his happiness, are all torn from him, overwhelmed with sadness and despair, he knows not whether to turn for relief. If, as is most natural for a creature in distress, he lifts his supplicating eyes to his maker, conscious ingratitude and disobedience to God, immediately check him: if he turn to his fellow-men, whom he has abused or neglected, consciousness of meriting their
contempt

contempt or averfion, difcourages him. If he feeks relief in his own mind, there, fhame, remorfe and felf-condemnation, muft overwhelm him.

But to the man whofe foul rejoices in his God, adverfity has nothing gloomy and terrible. Believing every thing in the world to be under the administration of God, and looking up to that God, as to an all-wife and benevolent father and friend, he welcomes every thing that comes from him. Perfuaded that the Father of Mercies, delighteth not needlefsly to *grieve* the children of men; and well knowing that he forefaw this impending affliction, and could eafily have prevented it: he concludes, that, fince it *is* come, it is come on fome errend of love.

> " Since all the downward tract of time,
> God's watchful eye furveys,
> O who fo wife to chufe our lot,
> To regulate our ways!

> Since none can doubt his equal love,
> Unmeasurably kind,
> To his unerring gracious will,
> Be every wish resign'd.
>
> Good, when he gives, supremely good,
> Nor less when he denies,
> E'en *crosses* from his sovereign hand,
> *Are blessings—in disguise.*"

O the sweetly powerful influences of love! Love can enable the sugar-doating child cheerfully to take the cup of *wormwood*, from the hand of the parent whom he loves. Love can cause the delicate woman to forget better days, and to smile in poverty and toil with the husband whom she loves. Aye, and if we loved God as we ought, none of his dealings would seem grievous to us. The very idea, that this or that affliction was brought on us by him, would sweetly reconcile us to it, and kindle in us a divine ambition to please him by the cheerfulness of our submission. Afflictions we should look on not as marks of God's

God's displeasure, but as certain evidences of his love—

" As many as I love, I chastise."——JEHOVAH.

" *I HAVE smitten you with blasting and mildew, your vineyards and your fig trees did the palmer worm devour.*"—JEHOVAH.

AND then the love that did this, makes this complaint, "*Yet ye have not returned to me.*"

" PESTILENCE *have I sent amongst you; I have made the smell of your dead to come up even in your nostrils.*"

AND then the same love that inflicted this wholesome chastisement repeats the complaint. O my brethren, see here the design and end of all God's chastisements! "*Yet have ye not returned to me.*"

THESE are the views in which the divine lover is taught to contemplate the afflictive dispensations of his God; not as the messengers of his wrath, but as the ministers of his mercy, and the great means of wisdom and virtue. Such views of God's adorable government, impart the most sensible consolation to every pious heart. They place the compassions of the universal Father, in the most endearing light. And these *afflictions*, which human follies render necessary; instead of estranging, do but the more closely attach a good man to his God. "*Although the fig tree shall not blossom, neither shall fruit be in the vine; the labour of the olive shall fail, and the fields shall yield no meat: yea, though the flock shall be cut off from the fold, and there shall be no herd in the stalls; yet, will I rejoice in the Lord, I will joy in the God of my salvation.*"

But a supreme love of God adds unspeakably to the happiness of life, because it raises us superior to the dread of death. To form a tolerable idea of the magnitude of this blessing, let us visit the death bed of him who is about to to depart without love or hope in his God.

BEHOLD him arrested by the strong arm of death, and stretched out hopeless and despairing on that last bed from which he is to rise no more. Art has done its all; the mortal malady mocks the power of medicine, and hastens with resistless impetuosity to execute its dreadful errand. See the thick gloom that covers his ghastly countenance, and the wildness and horror that glare on his rolling eye-balls! Whither now is fled that giddy thoughtlessness which marked his mad career through life? Where now are his scoffs, his sneers, his pleasantries on religion? Where are his boon companions who joined him in his dull profanity, and who applauded the keeness of his satire and the brilliancy of his wit? Alas! such scenes as these are not for them. To cheer the drooping spirits of wretchedness, and to administer

minister consolation to a dying friend is no employment of theirs. In far different scenes they are now forgetting their no longer entertaining friend, and their present alarming thoughts.

Unhappy Man! wherever he turns his eyes, he sees none but subjects of sorrow and distress. Forsaken by those whom he fondly called his friends; cut off from all the pleasures and cheerful pursuits of men, abandoned to the horrors of a dying chamber, with no sensations but those of a tortured body; no comforter but a guilty conscience, and no society but such as fills his troubled mind with shame and remorse; a weeping wife whom he has injured; children whose best interests he has neglected; servants whom he has treated with cruelty; and neighbours with whom he has long lived at shameful variance—Whither shall he look for help? If he look backward he sees nothing but scenes of of horror, a precious life mispent, an immortal soul neglected; and, O insupportable thought! his day of trial about to set forever. If he looks forward, he sees an offended God, a fearful reckoning, and an awful eternity. If he looks up to Heaven for mercy, conscious guilt depresses his spirits and overwhelms him with despair. Ah! what mortal scene can well be conceived more fraught with wretchedness! Shuddering, he stands upon the dreadful brink, afraid to die, and yet, alas! unable to live.

"*In that dread moment, how the frantic soul raves round the walls of her clay tenement; runs to each avenue and shrieks for help, but shrieks in vain: how wishfully she looks on all she's leaving, now no longer hers! a little longer, yet a little longer: O! might she stay to wash away her crimes. and fit her for her passage! Mournful sight! her very eyes weep blood; and every groan she heaves is big with horror;*

ror.; but the foe, like a staunch murderer, steady to his purpose, pursues her close through every lane of life, nor misses once the track, but presses on, till forced at last to the tremendous verge—at once she sinks."

BLAIR.

This, or very similar to this, is often the end of him who has lived without God in the world.

But turning from so distressing a scene, to its happy opposite, let us view the man who loves his God, and who enamoured with its beauty, and sensible of its blessed effects, has lived a life of piety and virtue. Let us behold him when about to leave this world of sorrow and suffering and to wing his way to that which is far better. Lo! the time is come that Israel, the lover of God, must die. The last sickness has seized his feeble frame. He perceives that the all conquering foe is at hand, but marks his approach without dismay. He

He is not afraid of death becaufe he fears God, *" and he who fears God has nothing elfe to fear."*

He is not afraid of death, becaufe it has long been his care to make a friend (the almighty and everlafting Jehovah), who fhall ftand by him in that awful hour. He is not afraid of death, becaufe he loves God above all things; and to him, to die, is to go to fee and live with God.

Is the poor hireling afraid of the earning, which is to refrefh him with repofe, and to rejoice him with his reward?

Is the foldier, covered with fcars and tired of wars alarms, afraid to hear the cry of victory? O no! delightful found, fweeter than mufic to his longing ear; it is the fignal to return to his native country, and to refign the din and dangers of war for the fweets and fafety of long coveted peace.

EVEN

Even so, to the good Christian this world is the field of hard, though glorious warfare. In the service, and under the eye of God, he is now fighting against the armies of his own fleshly lusts, and of his own malignant passions. Ever and anon, he hears the voice of his great Captain—*Persevere and thou shalt conquer; endure unto the end and thou shalt be crowned.* To him therefore the day of death is welcome as the *last day* of his toils and dangers. He is now going to exchange a long conflicting war for the blessings of everlasting peace: having fought *the good fight*, he is about to receive his wages, even *eternal life*, and to put on a crown of glory that shall never fade away. Sure that serene look, beaming all the sweetness of love and hope, bespeaks the already half-formed seraph; and the heaven, almost opened on his placid countenance, gives glorious evidence of his intended

intended journey. Soon bidding farewell forever to thefe realms of woe, and haunts of malignant beings, he fhall join the bleffed fociety of *angels and spirits of juft men made perfect.* There he fhall fee health blooming eternal on each immortal face, friendfhip fmiling on every glorified countenance, and a perfection of love forming a paradife of happinefs, unknown and unconceived by us who have dwelt in the tents of hatred.

But, above all, the fweeteft motives to refignation in death, he is now going to fee *him,* whom oftentimes with trembling joy, he has longed to fee, even his God, his firft, his laft, his only friend, the author of his being and of all his mercies. Shortly fhall he fee his glorious face unclouded with a frown, and hear from his ambrofial lips the language of approbation and affection— "*Well done good and faithful fervant.*"

PRAISING God for advancing him to such an height of honor, and for setting before him such an eternity of happiness: Praising God for all the loving kindnesses that have accompanied him through life, and especially for that greatest of all, the grace that brought him to repentance and a good life: earnestly exhorting his friends to that love of God, which now not only supports, but enables him even to triumph in this dying hour, an hour so alarming to the fears of nature: rejoicing in a sense of the pardon of his sins, and exulting in the hopes of the glory to be revealed, he breathes out his soul with these victorious words,—" *into thy hands, O God, I commend my spirit.*"

WELL may his friends, edified by such an example, cry out with weeping joy,—" *Who can count the rewards of wisdom, or number the fourth part of the blessings of virtue? Let us die the death of the*

the righteous, and let our latter end be like theirs."

But divine love not only renders life pleasant, and death peaceful, but it accompanies us into heaven, and there gives us to enjoy the moſt exquiſite pleaſures, that God himſelf can confer on happy ſouls: For there we ſhall always live in the preſence of God, the great fountain of all lovelineſs and glory, and ſhall love him with ten thouſand times more ardour than we now do, or even can imagine; for the longer we behold, the more we ſhall know him, and the more we know, the better we ſhall love him; and ſo through everlaſting ages, our love ſhall be extending and enrapturing itſelf with his infinite beauty and lovelineſs. Now love is the ſweeteſt and happieſt of all paſſions, and it is merely by accident that it is accompanied with any diſquieting or painful feelings. Either the perſon beloved is abſent,

which

which corrodes it with unquiet defire, or he is unhappy, or unkind, which imbitters it with grief; or he is fickle and inconftant, which inflames it with rage and jealoufy; but, feparated from all thefe difagreeable accidents, and it is all pure delight and joy.

But in heaven, our love of God will have none of thefe difquieting circumftances attending it; for there he will never be abfent from us, but will be continually entertaining our amorous minds with the profpect of his infinite beauties. There we fhall always feel his love to us in the moft fenfible and endearing effects, even in the glory of that crown which he will fet upon our heads, and in the ravifhing fweetnefs of thofe joys which he will infufe into our hearts. There we fhall experience the continuation of his love in the continued fruition of all that an everlafting heaven means, and be convinced,

as

as well by the perpetuity of his goodnefs to us, as well as by the immutability of his nature, that he is an unchangeable lover. And there we fhall find him a moft happy being, happy beyond the vafteft wifhes of our love; fo that we fhall not only delight in him, as he is infinitely lovely, but rejoice and triumph in him too as he is infinitely happy. For love unites the interefts, as well as the hearts of lovers, and gives to each, the joys and felicities of the other. So that in that blefled ftate we fhall fhare in the felicity of God proportionably to the degree of our love to him: For the more we love him, the more we fhall ftill efpoufe his happy intereft; and the more we are interefted in his happinefs, the happier we muft be, and the more we muft enjoy of it. Thus love gives us a real poffeffion and enjoyment of God; it makes us co-partners with him in himfelf, derives his happiness upon us, and makes it as really ours as his. So that God's happiness is, as it were, the common bank and treasury of all divine lovers, in which they have every one a share, and of which, proportionably to the degrees of their love to him, they do all draw and participate to all eternity. And could they but love him as much as he deserves, that is *infinitely*, they would be as infinitely blessed and happy as he is: For then all his happiness would be theirs, and they would have the same delightful sense and feeling of it, as if it were all transplanted into their own bosoms. God, therefore being an infinitely lovely, infinitely loving, and infinitely happy being, when we come to dwell forever in his blessed presence, our love to him can be productive of none but sweet and ravishing emotions; for the immense perfections it will then find in its object,

must

must necessarily refine it from all those fears and jealousies, those griefs and displeasures that are mingled with our earthly loves, and render it a most pure delight and complacency. So that when thus refined and grown up to the perfection of the heavenly state, it will be all heaven, it will be an eternal paradise of delights within us, a living spring whence rivers of pleasures will flow for evermore.

THESE, O man, are some of the golden fruits that grow upon the tree of divine love. Happy, therefore, is the man, beyond all expression of words, beyond all conception of fancy, happy is he who obtaineth this angelic virtue!

"*For the merchandise of it is better than the merchandise of silver, and the gain thereof than fine gold. She is more precious than rubies, and all the things that thou canst desire are not to be compared unto her. She is a tree of life to them that*

that lay hold upon her, and happy is every one that retaineth her."

Since a supreme love of God is the only true wealth of an immortal mind, O! with what diligence should we apply ourselves to obtain it! We are all ready enough to acknowledge our obligations to God, and to own that it is our duty to love him, but still complain of the difficulty that attends it. But let us remember that this difficulty is chargeable upon ourselves, and is the effect of our own shameful inconsideration. Taken up with the little cares of life, we neglect and forget God; hence, it is not surprising that we do not love him. Would we but often think of him, what he is in himself, and contemplate him in the full blaze of his wonderful and amiable perfections, we should be overwhelmed with delightful admiration of him, and easily take up the most exalted esteem and friendship for him. And
were

were we but frequently to confider him, what he is to us, how infinitely condefcending, generous and good, we fhould foon feel our hearts melting into all the tendernefs of love and gratitude. We, none of us think it hard to love the tender mother who brought us into the world, the fond father who fupplies our wants, or the attentive teacher who inftructs us in ufeful and ornamental knowledge; ah! why then fhould we think it hard to love our God? Did we but reflect, we fhould foon perceive that he is really and truly our mother, our father and our teacher; and that thofe whom we honor as fuch, are, properly fpeaking, only the inftruments of his goodnefs to us.

SYLVIA arrived to years of maturity, receives the addreffes of a young and accomplifhed lover. Sylvia blufhes and likes him. Youthful modefty caufes her to hefitate a while, yet, unable to

refift

refift fo much merit, fhe at length yields to the impulfe of a virtuous paffion and marries. In due feafon fhe becomes a mother. Now, what has Sylvia hitherto done for her child? The whole is the work of God. When he laid the foundations of the heavens and the earth, he had this child in view, and difpofed, from fo remote a period, a long chain of events, which were to terminate in his nativity. The time being come for the opening of this bud, he was pleafed to place it in Sylvia's womb, and took care himfelf to cherifh and unfold it.

That this child fhould love and honor his mother is what he certainly ought to do, for fhe has fuffered, if not for his fake, at leaft through him, the inconveniencies of pregnancy, and the pains of child-birth. But let him carry his grateful acknowledgments ftill higher, and not imitate thofe fuperftitious idolators, who, feeing the earth yearly covered

covered with corn, fruits and paſtures, ſtupidly worſhipped this blind inſtrument of the bounties of their Sovereign Lord, without ever thinking to praiſe the powerful arm from whence it derives its fruitfulneſs.

CHARLES loves his father Eugenis. Charles does well; but what has Eugenis done for Charles? Eugenis has not, it is true, reſembled that proud parent who beggars the reſt of his children in order to ſwell the fortune of an elder brother. Nor is he like that ſtern tyrannical father who never looks at his children but with fury, never ſpeaks to them but in paſſion, never inſtructs them but by threats, and corrects them like a butcher and a murderer. Nor yet does he act like Florimond, that unnatural father, who lives like a ſtranger in his own houſe; goes in and out, drinks, games, and ſaunters; meanwhile his neglected children grow up,
to

to the years of maturity; happy indeed if of themselves inclinable to virtue, they make any attainments in useful knowledge and accomplishments, or think of settling in the world; for as to his part, he never troubles his head about them. No, far unlike these, Eugenis is the best of parents; he spares no pains nor expence to render his son Charles an ornament and a blessing to his country. He accustoms him by times to a temperate diet, furnishes him with decent apparel, and charges the ablest masters with his instruction; he carefully teaches him his relation to God, and his obligations to that best of beings; and, at the same time, by precept and example, endeavours to inspire him with the love of justice, honor and industry. These are, to be sure, the dearest expressions of a father's love, and hard and detestable indeed would be Charles' bosom, if he could

could refuse to love such a parent; but let him remember, that all this comes ultimately from God; for we should always ascend to this original of blessings. When Eugenis watched for his son's preservation; it was God who preserved him; when he took care to instruct him, it was God who opened his understanding; and when he entertained him with the charms of virtue, it was God who excited him to love it.

" *The labourer digs the mine; the philosopher directs the work; but neither of them furnish the gold which it contains.*"

But what heart so hard as to resist the golden shafts of love, especially when coming from a friend that is far superior to us? If some good and mighty prince were to invite us to his court, and to treat us with all the tenderness of parental affection, should we not find it a very easy thing to love him? Now, has not this been the conduct of God our Maker? When we lay in all the obscurity of duſt, he ſent a meſſage of love, and called us into life, not the life of fluttering inſects, but of infant immortals. For us, and for our ſakes, he built this vaſt world; he covered it with the canopy of the heavens, and ſtored it with good things innumerable. At his command the ſun riſes to gladden us with the golden day; and the moon with ſilver beams to cheer the darkneſs of the night. He waters the hills from his ſecret chambers, and bids the clouds pour down their fattening ſhowers upon the earth. Thus he covers our tables with bread to renew our ſtrength, and with wine that makes glad our hearts.

But he has not only compaſſed us round, like ſo many fortunate iſlands, with a vaſt ocean of good things for our bodies; but he has likewiſe inſpired us with immortal minds, and has induced

induced them with the high capacities of *knowledge* and *love*, whereby, as on golden ladders, we may ascend to the perfection and happiness of celestial beings. And to gratify these our noble capacities, he has prepared for us a glorious heaven, and has furnished it with all the pleasures and delights that heavenly spirits can desire or enjoy. Besides all this, he has sent his own son from heaven to reveal to us the way thither, and to encourage us to return into it by dying for our sins, and thereby obtaining for us a public grant and charter of mercy and pardon, on condition of our return : and, as if all this were too little, he hath sent his spirit to us in the room of his son, to reside amongst us, and, as his vicegerent, to carry on this vast design of his love to us, to excite and persuade us to return into the way leading to heaven, and to assist us all along in
our

our good travels thither. Such wonderful care has he taken not to be defeated of this his kind intention to make us everlastingly happy. "*O that men would therefore love the Lord for his goodness, and declare the wonders that he doth for the children of men.*"

THAT these dear pledges of God's love may inspire our hearts with suitable returns of gratitude, we should often *reflect* on them, and spread them before our minds in all their endearing circumstances. We should frequently set our cold and frozen affections before these melting flames of his love, and never cease fanning the smoking flax until we feel the heavenly fire beginning to kindle in our bosoms.

AND, while we are seeking this *Israel* of *great price*, let us, as we hope for success, guard our *innocence*, as the trembling miser guards his hoarded gold. The bosom that burns with impure desires, fires, or that is corroded with malignant paffions, finds no delight in God. No, that is a happinefs referved only for the pure in heart, and for him who knows how to pity an offending brother.

AND, together with our own exertions, we fhould often implore the aid of all affifting heaven. To him, who alone knows its ineftimable worth, let our fervent prayers be conftantly afcending.

"*FATHER of life and love, thou God fupreme, O teach our hearts to love thee: For to whom, O Lord, fhall we give our hearts but to thee? Thou alone haft generoufly created them; thou alone haft infinitely deferved them; and thou alone canft completely and eternally fatisfy them.*"

THESE prefcriptions, faithfully obferved, will foon produce in our hearts that love, whofe joy paffeth all underftanding, that love, poffeffed of which, the poorest

poorest slave is passing rich; while without it, the sceptered monarch walks but in splendid poverty.

He who loves God is the alone wise, dignified and happy man. For he loves the only good that is worthy the affections of an immortal mind. He loves a friend who alone possesses almighty power to protect him, unerring wisdom to counsel him, and infinite love to bless him. He loves an immortal friend who can never die and forsake him, and an unchangeable friend who will never requite his love with neglect.

His love of God sweetens every duty, and makes the yoke of obedience to sit light. It heightens the smile of prosperity, and cheers the gloom of adversity. Blessings are doubly dear coming from such a friend; and afflictions not unwelcome, when looked on as tokens of his no less tender love. Under the languors of sickness he remembers, not without

without sacred comfort, that the end of his sufferings is at hand; and even when this earthly tabernacle of his flesh is pulling down, he is not disconsolate; he rejoices in the hope of that glorious house not made with hands, eternal in the heavens. There, far removed from all the miseries of this mortal life, advanced into the presence of him who made him, and accompanied by millions of loving and blessed spirits, he shall enjoy a happiness as far exceeding his expectations as his deserts:—
" A happiness which eye hath not seen nor ear heard, nor hath entered into the heart of man to conceive."

CHAP.

CHAP. II.

ON SOCIAL LOVE.

"*This only can the bless bestow,*
"*Immortal souls should prove,*
"*From one short word all pleasures flow,*
"*That blessed word is—*LOVE."

PROUD.

THE first fruits of a creature's love are due to God, as to his Creator and the author of all his good; the second are due to men, as to his brethren and fellow sharers in the bounties of their common parent. Having in the preceding chapter, demonstrated the importance of loving God, proceed we in this to consider the beauty and blessedness of *social love*.

To

To be careffed and beloved by all around us, is one of the deareft wifhes of the human heart. It is a natural, it is a laudable wifh. Great pains have been taken, and infinite expence incurred to attain this coveted honor, and yet the greater part never attain it, merely through defect of love on their own part. Let beauty, wit, gold, &c. boaft and do all they can, yet will it be found in the end, that

"In fpite of all the dull miftaken elves,
"They who wou'd make us love, muft love, them-
"felves."

Love is the univerfal charm. It poffeffes a beauty that wins and ravifhes every heart. A fingle fpark of it in generofity of dealing excites our admiration; a glimpfe of it in courteous behaviour fecures to a man our efteem, and fweetly endears him to us. How charming is the countenance that is brightened by the fmiles of love! How fweet the voice that is tuned by the melody

melody of love! How gladdening to the heart, the beams that sparkle from the eye of love! Indeed love, or goodness, which is but another name, is the only amiable thing in nature. Power and wealth may be respected, wit and beauty may be admired, but if separated from goodness, they neither deserve nor can command our love: For the worst and most wretched of beings possess them in a very high degree. The prince of darkness has more power, and tyrannizes over more slaves by far than the Great Turk. One devil may have more wit than all the Achitophels in the world, and yet, with all his wit, he is very odious and miserable. And such, in proportion, is every one who partakes in his accursed disposition of hatred and malice.

See how Pandorus is beloved and caressed. Is it because of his honesty? This virtue only gains our esteem, but does

does not captivate the heart. Is it becaufe he is beneficent and friendly? Many who are fo fond of his company have no need of his affiftance. Is it becaufe he is gay, humorous, and entertaining? This would render him agreeable, only when gaiety is feafonable. No, he is more beloved than any other man in the world, only becaufe he is the moft *affectionate* man in it. He feems to live but to pleafe, to oblige, and to ferve his friends. If he find out what will pleafe you, he prevents your defires, and does it with fuch an air of cheerfulnefs, that, while he has no other view than to oblige you, he feems to follow nothing but his own choice and inclinations. This charming complaifance of Pandorus was not learned in the fchool of the world; but is the rich fruit of his genuine benevolence. Hence it renders him equally endearing and equally agreeable, at all times,

times, and to all ranks. He is not a sycophant to the great, and scornful or negligent of the poor; he does not treat you to-day as a *dear friend,* and to-morrow *knows you not,* but *uniformly* his looks and manners are those of the man who considers both the rich and the poor as his brethren. If you love like Pandorus, and like him take a pleasure in contributing to the happiness of others, I will answer for the friendship of all who know you; this is a perfection that will engage people at all times, in all places, and on all occasions.

But love not only renders us thus dear and desireable to others; but it spreads the sunshine of sweetest peace over our own minds. It delivers us from the tyranny of all those bad passions which make us miserable. Like a golden curb it checks the fierceness of anger, that dangerous storm and hurricane of the soul. A man can hardly be be incensed against those whom he tenderly loves: an accidental neglect, a hasty word, a small unkindness, will not agitate a loving spirit, much less work it up to hateful *fire-eyed* fury.

It banishes envy, that severely just vice which never fails to punish itself; for it is impossible to repine at the wealth or prosperity, at the virtue or fame of him whom we cordially love. It excludes revenge, that cruel canker of the heart; for who can indulge bitter resentments, or form dark designs of evil against him whom he tenderly loves, and in whose good he heartily delights?

It subdues ambition and avarice, those aspiring painful passions. For who could domineer over those whom he loves, and whose honor he tenders as his own? Who could extort from and impoverish those whom he earnestly wishes and would gladly see to prosper?

A competence will seem like abundance to him who lives as among brethren, taking himself but for one among the rest, and can as ill endure to see them want as himself.

It is in the prevalence of such bad passions as these, that human misery chiefly consists. Love is their only sovereign antidote. It alone subdues and expels their fatal poison, and thus restores health and happiness to our long tortured bosoms. Love, like a celestial queen, walks before, meekness and gentleness follow as her eldest daughters, while joy and peace, with all the sister graces, make up the immortal retinue.

But love preserves us not only from our own, but from the malignant passions of others. Like sweetest music, it has power to sooth the savage breast, to melt hearts of flint, and to tame the fiercest spirits. Its mild and serene countenance, its soft and gentle spirit its courteous and obliging manners, its fair dealing, its endearing converſation, its readineſs to do good ſervices to any man, is the only charm under heaven to diſarm the bad paſſions of men, and to guard our perſon from aſſault, our intereſt from damage, and our reputation from ſlander. For who can be ſo unnatural as to hate the man who loves us and is ever ready to do us good? What wretch, what demon, can find in his heart to be a foe to him who is a warm friend to all? The vileſt ſinner cannot be ſo vile, ſo deſtitute of goodneſs. *If you love thoſe who love you what reward have you, do not even ſinners the ſame?*

Of this wonderful power of love, to convert foes into friends, we have many pleaſing examples in holy writ. Eſau was a rough man, and exceedingly angry with his brother Jacob, and yet how eaſily did Jacob's meek and affectionate behaviour overcome him! "*Eſau ran*

ran to meet *Jacob, and fell on his neck and kissed him, and they wept.*"

Saul was possessed with a furious envy and spite against David. Yet what acknowledgments did David's generous dealing extort from him?—

"*Is this thy voice my son David? Thou art more righteous than I, for thou hast rewarded me good, whereas I have rewarded the evil; behold I have played the fool, and erred exceedingly.*"

Though gratitude is not so common a virtue as it ought to be, yet the remembrance of his former kindnesses often surrounds a good man in distress, with many warm friends and generous comforters. Is he in danger, who will not defend him? Is he falling, who will not uphold him? Is he slandered, who will not vindicate him?

Love disposes us to put to their proper uses every blessing that may fall to our lot; while, *without it*, the most splendid

splendid advantages that we could desire, the largest fortunes and brightest parts, will become vain and fruitless, if not pernicious and destructive to us. For, what is our reason worth if it serve only to contrive little sorry designs for ourselves? What is wit good for, if it be spent only in making sport, or creating mischief? What signifies wealth, if it be uselessly hoarded up, or vainly thrown away on the lusts of one poor worm? What is our credit but a mere puff of air, if we do not give it substance by making it an engine of doing good? What is our virtue itself, if buried in obscurity it yield no benefit to others by the lustre of its example, or by its real influence? If these advantages minister, only to our own particular pleasure or profit, how mean and inconsiderable they appear!

But under the management of love, see what worth and importance they assume.

fume. Our wealth becomes the bank from which the weeping widow, the indigent young tradesman, and the helpless orphan, draw the supply of their wants. Our wit is employed to expose the deformities of vice, and to paint virtue in her loveliest colours. Our knowledge is applied to instruct the ignorant, to admonish the guilty, and to comfort the wretched. Thus love enables us to lay out our talents in so excellent a manner as to secure those inestimable blessings—the love of God, the friendship of mankind, and all the exquisite pleasures of doing good. How great then is the worth of love, since without it the goods even of the wealthiest are but temporal and transient, such as too often prove dangerous snares and baneful poisons, and are at best but impertinent baubles.

Love gives worth to all our apparent virtues, insomuch, that without it no quality

quality of the heart, no action of life is valuable in itself or pleasing to God. Without love, what is courage, but the boldness of a lion or the fierceness of a tyger? What is meekness but the softness of a woman, or the weakness of a child? What is politeness, but the grimace of a monkey, or the fooleries of a fop? What is justice, but passion or policy? What is wisdom but craft and subtilty? Without love, and what is faith but dry opinion? What is hope but blind presumption? What is almsgiving but ostentation? What is martyrdom but stubborness? What is devotion but a mockery of God? What is any practice, how specious soever in itself, or beneficial to others, but the effect of selfishness and pride? *" Though I have faith so that I could remove mountains, and have not love, I am nothing. Though I give all my goods to feed the poor,*

poor, and have not love, it profiteth me nothing."

But love sanctifies every action, and converts all that we do into virtue. It is true bravery indeed, when a man, out of love to his neighbour, and a hearty desire to promote his good, encounters dangers and difficulties. It is genuine meekness, when a man out of love, and an unwillingness to hurt his neighbour, patiently puts up with injuries. It is politeness indeed, when cordial affection expresses itself in civil language, respectful manners, and obliging actions. It is excellent justice, when a man regarding his neighbour's case as his own, does to him as he would have it done to himself. It is admirable wisdom, which studies to promote our neighbour's welfare. It is a noble faith, which, working by love, produces the rich fruits of obedience. It is a solid hope, which is grounded on that everlasting lafting bafis of love which never fails. It is a fincere alms, which not only the hand but the heart reaches out. It is an acceptable facrifice, which is kindled by the holy fire of love. It is an hallowed devotion which is offered up from a heart pure and benevolent like the being whom it adores.

Love is a grand inftrument of our happinefs, becaufe it alone renders fweet and pleafant all the duties which we owe to our neighbour. All agree, that the fecond great bufinefs of men in this life is to learn to love one another. And fince the conftant performance of kind and generous fervices to each other, tends moft effectually to fan the flame of love, our heavenly Father is perpetually calling on us to perform thofe good offices to our brethren. He commands *the ftrong to bear the burdens of the weak, the rich to abound in good works to the poor, the poor to be cheerfully obliging to the rich,* and all of us to exercise meekness, gentleness, hospitality, justice, honor, truth, &c. Such sentiments and works of beneficence and love, make a considerable part of our duties, duties that occur every *day* and *hour* of our lives. To perform these with alacrity and pleasure must add greatly to our happiness, because, since they occur so frequently, if we have but the art to turn them into pleasures, our whole life must be one continued round of pleasure. Whereas, on the contrary, if we take no delight in them, we stand a fair chance to lead very uneasy lives; as we shall be continually called on by duties which we cannot perform without reluctance, nor yet neglect without much vexation and regret.

Would we have this, our field of trial, to become a garden of pleasantness? Let us love. Love is the great wonder.

wonder-worker. It converts duties into delights, and penances into pleasures. Are you wealthy? In making you so, heaven kindly intended for you the joy of acting as the friend and benefactor of the poor. That you may be sensible how essential love is to the cheerful discharge of the duties of beneficence, turn your eyes towards Dives: In him you behold one of the wealthiest of the sons of fortune. His cellars, his barns, his coffers, are all bursting out with abundance; but his heart possesses not one spark of love. Alas! the sad consequences of his lacking *this one thing needful*. Hence, though possessed of wealth sufficient to enable him, like the good angel of his neighbourhood, to scatter blessings around him on at least fifty needy families; he loses the joy, and they the benefit of such noble charities. Destitute of love, Dives takes no delight, even in feeding the hungry,

in

in cloathing the naked, or in soothing the sorrows of sickness and poverty. Unhappy Dives! Works of love which blessed angels would prefer to their nectar and ambrosia, are set before thee, but thou hast no relish for them. Dives keeps a splendid table, has vast apartments, rich furniture, costly jewels, a large number of servants, and sumptuous equipages; and that is enough for him; his poor childish fancy has no idea of any thing superior.

But see the noble and excellent Demophilus. Demophilus possesses an estate not inferior to that of Dives; but his estate, though ample, is not half so ample as his heart. Demophilus denies himself all the pomps and superfluities of life, in order that he may swell the tide of his liberality to the poor. It were an endless, though pleasing task, to relate how many friendless little children he has educated, how many

many poor young tradesmen he has set up in good business; and how many helpless old persons, provided for by his bounty, are now spending the evening of their days in peace and comfort. Every day is to Demophilus a day of happiness, because it is spent in offices of kindness to those whom love has taught him to view in the endearing light of relations; and, in serving whom, he acts with all the alacrity of a brother. Thus love employs him in such good works as yield the purest pleasures while he is engaged in them, and the remembrance of which will be a well of sweetest waters springing up in his bosom to eternal life.

ARE you a poor man? You will find love to be equally essential to your haphapiness. Love will not only preserve you from all the pangs of envy and discontent; those infernal vipers which pry on the vitals of too many of our poor brethren! But it will enable you to look with the joy of a brother on the superior prosperity of your neighbour. It will inspire you with that sublimest devotion, prayers for your wealthy neighbour, that he may be sensible of the blessings he possesses in possessing wealth and power, that he may be thankful for them, and put them to such good use as at once to please the supreme giver, to win the gratitude of the poor, and to fill his own heart with joy.

Are you in debt to your neighbour? Then it nearly concerns you to love him. I will not indeed say, that if you do not love, you will never pay your debts, for a sense of honor may incline you, as it does many who are destitute of love, to be honest; but this I will say, that if you love your neighbour, you will pay him with much more certainty and satisfaction than you otherwise wife could. If you love your neighbour, you will not be able to run in debt to him, when you forsee that you can never pay him.

A CERTAIN lawyer—a case in point—made application to a certain hair-dresser for a wig. The generous tradesman, who was just about to sit down to dinner, invited his customer to take pot-luck with him. After having made a plentiful repast, and emptied the second bowl, "*Now Sir,*" said the benevolent shaver, addressing his guest, "*I'll make you as handsome a wig as ever graced the head of a counsellor.*"—"*No, that you shall not.*"—"*Hie! what's the matter? Did you not come to bespeak a wig?*"—"*True, I did, but I have altered my mind. You are so clever a fellow that I have a great liking for you, and this makes me scorn to take an advantage of you: For were you to make me a wig, I do not know that I should ever be able to pay you for*

for it."—What a generous thing must love be, since a few feathers of it only could thus bear a man up above a dishonest action! Would God, that not only all lawyers, but that all men also had more of it!

To the man who loves not, the payment of his debts is often a great penance. Avaro owes 500 guineas—500 guineas! Avaro had as lieve it were 500 drops of his heart's blood. To-morrow is the day of payment; a sad day to Avaro! Avaro goes with a heavy heart to his strong box to take one more view of his dear poor guineas. He takes them up in his hands; he hugs them to his breast:—"*Sweet precious gold, and must I part with you! Dear delight of my eyes and joy of my heart, must I to-morrow resign you for ever!*" Avaro sighs piteously, and locking them up again in his box, goes out groaning like

like one who follows his firſt born to the grave.

Now turn your eyes to a very different character; I mean Benevolus. It is love only that makes the difference. Benevolus owes a ſum of money to his neighbour Agathos. Benevolus poſſeſſes not only that delicate ſenſe of honor, and that nice regard to reputation, thoſe laudable motives to duty which animate all men of honor; but he feels ſome of a ſweeter and ſtill ſtronger nature.—Benevolus loves his neighbour Agathos; hence he takes an intereſt in his welfare. Agathos, in lending this money, ſhewed a confidence in Benevolus. Benevolus is eager to evince that it was well-founded. Agathos, may by this time be *wanting* his money,—Benevolus feels an anxiety to replace it. Benevolus has reaſon to believe that it would be a pleaſure to Agathos to receive it—Benevolus haftens to give him that pleafure.

"I once, faid the charming Pulcheria, owed a neighbouring woman, a fum: On going to her houfe to pay it, I met one of her daughters, whofe drefs fhewed a tattered wardrobe: my heart rejoiced that the fupply of their wants was at hand: and had I, continued the dear girl, been in fufficient circumftances, nothing would have made me happier than to have owed them ten times as much."—O for more love; more love! Without this, there can be not only no pleafure, but indeed no *fteadinefs* in the payment of debts.— Great ftrefs I know has been laid on what is called a fenfe of honor: But a mere man of honor is an unfafe debtor. In thofe corrupted countries, where the *laws* and *fafhions* are not very decidedly in favour of juftice, men of honor have been

been found to fit perfectly eafy under the weight of their debts.

MISOCHRISTIS is a man of honor; but he lives in a country where it happens not to be the *fafhion* for men of honor to pay their debts under three or four years. Mifochriftis, you fee, is furrounded by a croud of creditors, who are importunate with him for their money. Often had he avoided them before by making his fervants deny him; but, unfortunately, that ftratagem would not anfwer to day, for they poped in upon him before his ufual hour of rifing. He at firft determined not to ftir out of his chamber; but they as obftinately determined not to ftir until they faw him. He then ordered his fervant to tell them that he was indifpofed and could fpeak to no body; but the news of his indifpofition did not foften them in the leaft :—See him they muft. Whereon he fent word that he would
furrender,

surrender, and immediately comes to a parley.

"How now, gentlemen," says he, "can't a person be sick in his own house? Give me leave to tell you, that you don't behave handsomely.

"What have you to say, Mr. Rhedon? You made me a coach I fancy about three years ago; and have I not paid you twenty pistoles on account? Indeed you are vastly to be pitied! Go, go, don't be afraid of your money; no body loses any thing by me. See there is an honest man who has been my baker these six years; he knows how to behave himself to a person of my distinction; he has had great patience, and he shall not be a sufferer by it. Mr Rhedon, your servant,—I have something to say to these gentlemen,—you will call again.

"My

"My good friend, Artopolus, I have really a regard for you: You ferve me extremely well. How do you manage to make fuch good bread as you fend me? 'Tis excellent; there can be no fault found with fuch bread. Let me fee what it is I owe you? Two thoufand three hundred and forty-fix livres—That's juft what I owe you.—Well, I fhall not examine your account; I don't queftion but it is right. Two thoufand three hundred and odd livres. I fhall be able to pay you.—Well, Mr. Artopolus, the firft money I receive fhall be yours. You fhall not be at the trouble of coming for it; 'tis not reafonable you fhould;—why man 'tis you who keep me alive.

"So, here is my wine merchant:— I have longed for an opportunity, my friend, to take you to tafk. You know full well, Mr. Vintner, that you

"you have a pleasure in poisoning me
"with your wine. What the devil is
"it you put into it? I cannot drink
"three bottles but it deprives me of
"my understanding; and yet it is mo-
"ney you want—Go about your busi-
"ness—go; people who expect to be
"paid never serve their customers in
"that manner. You shall have no
"money till every body else is paid, if
"it were only to teach you to sell good
"wine.

"As for you, Monsieur Guillaumet,
"I am quite ashamed to have been so
"long without paying you. I am sen-
"sible of all the complaints you have
"against me. You have cloathed me
"and my whole family these five years,
"and I have not as yet paid you a sous.
"I promised to pay you towards the
"end of the last year, but I disappoint-
"ed you.—Is not that all you have to
"say to me? You know me very well,
"Monsieur

"Monsieur Guillaumet; do you imagine I could be so cruel as to let you be all this time out of your money, after you had disbursed such considerable sums for my use, if my tenants did but pay me? I must be a great villain if I could behave after that manner: But they will pay me by and by, and then you shall have your money.—Your servant,—Give me leave to speak to that gentlewoman.

"Good morrow, Mrs. Pernelle, I suppose you are come to demand your money for those thirty pieces of linen which I had of you two years ago? Well, I cannot pay you very soon. You see what a number of people I have promised already. But you can afford to wait a little. You are well to pass!"—"No, Sir, you are mistaken, my circumstances are very indifferent."—"Oh, so much
"the

"the worfe, my good miftrefs: when people cannot afford to give credit, they fhould never pretend to fell.

"As to the reft of you, my good friends," fays Mifochriftis, addreffing himfelf to thofe creditors who had not as yet received audience: "I fancy I don't owe you any great matters. You fee I am endeavouring to regulate my affairs. Give me a little more time; and if I can do no better at prefent, I will at leaft look over and fettle your accounts."

As foon as Mifochriftis had finifhed thefe words, he flew from them like lightening, leaving his creditors fo aftonifhed at his impudence, that he was quite out of their hearing before they had recollected themfelves sufficiently to make him a reply.

But if men of honor have been bad pay-mafters, becaufe punctuality was unfafhionable, they have been found equally ly fo in thofe happy play-times, when their good old mafter, the LAW, fell drowfy, and took no notice of his pupils actions.

YOUNG Adraftus, hard run for money, determines to try his friends. He goes to Agathocles, and in the bated breath and whifpering humblenefs of a borrower, begs the loan of a thoufand guineas.—A good round fum! But the benevolent Agathocles, a ftranger to fufpicion, grants the loan. Adraftus pockets the money and rides off, the happieft man in the world. For three years the good Agathocles got nothing from Adraftus but empty promifes and forrowful details of difappointments and lofes. At length a war breaks out, and the country wanting money, the prefs is converted into a mint, and paper dollars are ftruck off by the ream. Thefe the legiflator pronounces to be of equal value with gold and filver, and threatens trouble to the tory that shall refuse them as such. "*Hurra for us debtors,*" is now the cry. Blessed times! Whole caravans of honest men are now in motion to pay their debts. Adrastus joins the happy throng; and taking a witness with him, waits on the good old Agathocles, whose generous loan of a *thousand guineas*, he pays off with half a quire of paper currency—worth about £. 40.

Alas! poor honor! when severed from the love of God, and of man, what art thou but an empty name! Had Adrastus loved his God, could he thus have despised that golden precept which enjoins him—*to do unto others as he would that others should do unto him?*—Had Adrastus loved the generous Agathocles, could he have thus requited him evil for good—could he have thus repayed the noblest friendship with the basest

basest ingratitude?—Let the following true story reply.

A YOUNG gentleman, whom we shall call Leander, had the good fortune to be born of parents, who well knew that happiness consists rather in the good qualities of the heart, than in the rich contents of the strong box. He was therefore early taught to look on the love of God and of his neighbour, as the best wealth that man or angel can possess. His progress in virtue was equal to the fondest expectations of his parents. Truth, honor and goodness, shone so conspicuously in all his conduct, that to love him, one needed but to know him. At the age of three and twenty he lost his father; and possessing but a very small fortune, he resolved to go into trade. Leander had five or six mercantile friends, each of whom throwing in a couple of hundred pounds worth of goods, made him up a pretty assortment.

assortment. With great alacrity he entered upon this new employment; but, as it would seem, merely to evince the error of those parents, who think that religion alone is sufficient to make their children happy. His father had taken great pains to fit him for heaven; but had not sufficiently instructed him to make his way good here on earth. He had scarcely ever told Leander, that though it be happiness to love, it is still virtue to be prudent; and, that to mingle the *harmlessness of the dove with the wisdom of the serpent*, and to *take heed of men*, even while he *loves them*, are commandments of the Great Teacher himself. He had hardly ever mentioned to Leander, the importance of receipts, vouchers, and written contracts; nor related to him the many sad instances of unsuspecting goodness snared and ruined by insidious villainy; and how often, for want of receipts,

the

the beſt men have been compelled to a ſecond payment of debts that have kept their noſes to the grindſtone half their lives after. No; but to conſider all men as the children of God, and co-heirs of glory; to love them as him-ſelf, and to *think evil of no man*—theſe were the only ſentiments which Lean-der was taught: Theſe he carried with him behind the counter. Leander was ſoon found out to be a *fine young man!* every body admired his goods, and wiſhed to buy if they could but have a little credit. Leander anticipated every wiſh, and credited every body.

IN a very ſhort time, out of a thou-ſand pounds worth of goods, he had not a remnant left. His rivals were fit to burſt with ſpleen and envy at ſuch prodigious ſales; while his friends aſ-cribed ſuch ſingular ſuccefs to divine interpoſition. At the appointed time his creditors demanded their money.

The too credulous Leander was not prepared to pay. Unable to wait longer, they feized on his little patrimony, and threw him into prifon. Cruel parents, who thus expofe your children uncovered by the fhield of prudence, to the *fiery darts* of fraud and villainy! O remember that the want of prudence, is too often, even in the beft men, fucceeded by the want of virtue; and that, in many inftances, the devil himfelf afks not an abler advocate for *vice* than *poverty*. Happily for Leander, his virtue was full grown, and of a good conftitution. He did not, as thoufands have done, curfe that eafinefs of nature, that benevolence of fentiment, which had duped and betrayed him; he did not vow eternal war againft his fpecies, and refolve to practife in future the fame arts which had wrought his ruin. No! fraud and injuftice now appeared to him hateful as the hags of hell.

While,

While, by contrast, his love of virtue was exalted to adoration. To have deceived, though unintentionally, and thence to have injured his patrons, caused Leander much grief; but it was grief unimbittered by the gall of guilt. To have discovered such a want of virtue and humanity among men, excited emotions, but they were the emotions of compassion, not of resentment. Still *his prayers and his benevolence went up before God.* After fifty days confinement, the still virtuous Leander was discharged from prison, and from all legal obligation to pay his former debts. He then went round again among his debtors; many of whom affected by his pathetic remonstrances, discharged their accounts. With this money, purchasing a small assortment of goods, he entered a second time into trade, and with becoming caution. At the expiration of five years, having saved enough for

for that purpofe, he haftened up to town to pay off his former debts, and to evince the divinity of that love, which cannot be happy while it *owes any man* any thing. He called together his former creditors to a tavern, where, by his orders, a handfome dinner was prepared for them. He received them with the utmoft cordiality, and, without having as yet gratified their curiofity as to the occafion of the meeting, he politely preffed them to fit down to dine. On turning up their plates, every man beheld in a heap of fhining gold, the full amount, principal and intereft, of his former claim againft Leander.

> " Lord, who's the happy man that may
>   " To thy bleft courts repair?
> " Not ftranger like to vifit them,
>   " But to inhabit there.
> " 'Tis he who to his vows and truft,
>   " Has ever firmly ftood;
> " And tho' he promife to his lofs,
>   " He makes his promife good."

WE

We have been copious on this part of our subject, for a very plain reason: the payment of our debts is a duty that occurs so frequently, that whatever tends to make it a pleasure, must consequently add *greatly* to our happiness; and have abundantly shewn it is love, and love alone that can make honesty at all times a pleasure.

But there are many other duties, of equal importance to our own, and to the happiness of society, to the cheerful performance of which, love is as indispensibly necessary. This man's avarice may claim a part of our estate; or that man's unprovoked rage may insult our person, or slander our name; now, to bear all this with temper, and to negociate so discreetly with these our ungenerous neighbours, as to disarm their passions, and to make an honorable and lasting peace, is certainly a most desireable event; but it is an event which
nothing

nothing but almighty love can accomplish. And through defect of this love, how frequently have we seen the slightest incroachments, or provocations to stir up such horrid passions, in the bosoms of neighbours, and to hurry them into such shameful excesses of injury and revenge, as have ended in the destruction of each others souls, bodies, and estates!

Let the real history of goodman Gruff and his neighbour Grub, elucidate this melancholy truth.

These two men, whose fortunes were ample, lived near neighbours to each other; so near, that their lands, unmoved by the passion of their owners, lay and slept together in the most friendly embraces. That good being who had thus appointed their lots together in the same pleasant places, had unquestionably intended, that they should learn from their own experience, how happy

happy a thing it is for brethren to dwell together in unity. But alas! the ways of peace they knew not, for they were both ſtrangers to love; and, by natural confequence, both proud, felfifh, irafcible and vindictive. On a refurvey of his plantation, goodman Gruff found that his neighbour Grub had about two acres and a quarter of his ground in poffeffion.

No fooner had he made this *important difcovery*, than he fent orders to Mr Grub, and not in the moſt gentle terms, inſtantly to remove his fences, from that fpot of ground, or he fhould adopt meafures to compel him. From no friend on earth, would Mr. Grub have brooked fuch a meffage; but from Gruff, it was altogether infupportable. A reply, fuch as pride and hatred could dictate, was immediately made. A law fuit, of courfe, commenced.

THIS

This produced the effect that usually attends law-suits,—"a death unto friendship, and a new birth unto hatred." Every expence incurred in the course of the suit inflamed their mutual hatred; for they never failed to set down these expences to the account of each others roguery: They never deigned to salute, or to exchange a word; and, if accident at any time threw them into the same company, they cast such eyes of death on one another, and were so pointedly brutal in their manners, as to shock all who were not lost to humanity. To be threatened with the loss of two acres of land, or to have that much withheld, though each possessed many more than they could cultivate, was enough in such sordid souls, to awaken the most deadly passions. These were soon communicated to the rest of their families. The wives and daughters, could not, even at church, treat each other

with

with common civility; and the sons often disgraced themselves in bloody battles. Nor was this all, for their poor unoffending cattle, their hogs and horses, who, *poor things!* knew not the right leg from the left, were made to feel the sad effects of this unnatural strife: For, if carelessly wandering in quest of grass or roots, their homely fare, they happened in luckless hour, to stray within the hostile lines, straight a troop of angry slaves, with worrying dogs and furious stones, attacked them: or slily taking and loading them with yokes, doomed them to waste full many a day in woe and pain.

"*Cursed be their anger, for it was fierce, and their wrath, for it was cruel. O my soul! come not thou into their secret, unto their assembly; mine honor, be not thou united!*" JACOB.

Thus we see men, though born to walk with angels high in salvation, and the clims of bliss, acting, because destitute of love, just as if they were candidates for the society of infernal spirits!

A stranger to the origin of this shameful contest, would reasonably have supposed, from the fury with which it was conducted, that the actors in it, expected some signal advantages from it. "Surely," would he have said, " vast fields of fertile earth, with migh- " ty forests, and flocks and herds, with " heaps of golden treasure, must de- " pend on this important suit." But what would have been his astonishment, on finding, that the dear bought purchase of two acres of poor land, was the whole extent of their hopes!

"*Verily, man without love is as the wild ass's colt, and stupid as the beast that perisheth.*"

But

But to return to our litigious farmers, whom we left juſt engaged in a ſuit, Gruff againſt Grub, for two acres and a quarter of land, held and cultivated by the latter, but found by a reſurvey to belong to the former. The caſe ſeemed ſufficiently ſimple, and, as was generally thought, would ſoon be knocked off the doquet, and with but ſmall damages. But being found, as generally happens, much more complicated than it had at firſt appeared; it was kept ſo long in the different courts in which it had the fortune to be tried, that goodman Gruff was often heard to ſay, that " though he had gained " his ſuit, yet, through loſs of time, " neglect of buſineſs, tavern charges, " and extra fees to lawyers, he had " expended at leaſt one hundred half- " joes." While poor Grub, obliged to carry on ſo long a ſuit with monies borrowed on an exorbitant premium,

incurred

incurred a debt which coft him the whole tract, together with the two acres and a quarter which he had fo obftinately defended.

" *Blessed are the meek, for they ſhall inherit the earth.*"

Had thefe unfortunate men but loved, they might have lived happy. Like good Job's children, " *they would have gone and feaſted in their houſes each man his day, and ſent and called for his neighbour to eat and to drink with him.*" And then having his heart warmed and expanded with generous love, had goodman Gruff difcovered that his neighbour held unknowingly an acre or two of his land, he would have fcorned to notice it.

Ask the benevolent old Ralph, whether he would thus have threatened and perfecuted his neighbour Paul for a couple of acres? Obferve how he ſhakes his venerable locks, and, with a countenance

tenance strongly marking his abhorrence of such a thought, thus replies:—

"No, my friend, two acres of land
"should never have set me and my
"neighbour Paul at variance. Forty
"years have we lived near each other,
"and, thank God, it has been forty
"years of peace and friendship. Paul
"appears to me now like a brother;
"and the affection that I have for him,
"gives me a double enjoyment of what
"I have, because of the pleasure I find
"in communicating of it to him. If I
"take a hive, he is sure to receive a
"plate of the choicest comb. If I kill
"a fat mutton, the best quarter is sent
"to him. His company heightens my
"joys, his counsel and assistance lessen
"the weight of my sorrows. Toge-
"ther we enjoy the good things of
"this life, and together we often con-
"verse about the happiness of that bet-
"ter life to come. Now, shall I mar

"all

"all this sweet heavenly peace, and
"plunge myself into hellish hatred and
"strife, by quarrelling with my good
"friend Paul on account of two acres of
"ground? No, no, no; sooner than see
"that hated day, let these eyes be closed
"for ever; and let my grey hairs go
"down with joy to the grave! Take
"two acres of land from Paul? O how
"gladly would I give him a thousand!"

But supposing, Father Ralph, that instead of the gentle Paul, it had been your destiny to dwell in the neighbourhood of the churlish Mr. Gruff, how would you have relished his orders to relinquish two acres of your land?

"Why, I would have endeavoured
"an accommodation, by proposing a
"reference of our matter to some
"of our well informed and impartial
"neighbours."

But,

But, what if he had replied, that since by the late variation of the compass, the limits of his tract were so enlarged as to take in those two acres of yours, he claimed them by virtue of the law, and would have nothing to do with arbitrators?

"What would I have done? Why,
"I would have pitied him—from the
"bottom of my heart would I have
"pitied him for such a sentiment.
"And on taking my leave, would
"have addressed him in such words
"as these:—Neighbour Gruff, the good,
"for which you seem so ready to
"contend, deserves not to be put in
"the scale against the numerous evils
"of a law-suit. Let famished sea-
"men quarrel and fight for a mor-
"sel of bread, or draw lots for each
"others lives, but for us who live
"in a land so thickly strewed with
"the blessings of heaven, that we
need

"need but stretch forth the hand of industry and we shall gather abundance—for us to go to law for a slip of ground, were a reproach to us, both as men and as christians. I feel, neighbour Gruff, that love and peace are the greatest blessings of life, and, well knowing that law-suits are no friend to those, but, on the contrary, their most mortal enemies, I wish never to have any thing to do with law-suits—I mean on such trifling occasions. Therefore, for the sake of God, the lover of peace, and for our mutual good, I cheerfully compliment you with these two acres for which you are so ready to go to law with me. And I think my heart gives me comfortable assurance that I shall never want them."

"BLESSED *are the peace makers, for they shall be called the children of God.*"

LOVE

Love adds greatly to the happiness of man, because it puts us in possession and gives us the enjoyment of every thing that is good and desireable in this life. By it, we may, without greedy avarice, or its cares and drudgeries, swim in tides of wealth. Without proud ambition or any of its difficulties and dangers, we may ascend to the highest feats of honor: without sordid voluptuousness, or its diseases and disgust, we may bask in the lap of true pleasures; without its pride, luxury or sloth, or any of its snares and temptations, we may feast at the table of prosperity. We may pluck the richest fruits of science and learning, without the pain of laborious study: and we may taste the sweets of virtue and goodness without their toils. For, are not all these things ours, if we make them so, by finding much delight and satisfaction in them? Does not out neighbour's wealth

wealth enrich us, if we are happy in his poffeffing and ufing it? Does not his preferment advance us, if our spirit rifes with it into a cordial complacency? Does not his pleafure delight us, if we are pleafed with his enjoyment of it? Does not his profperity blefs us, if our hearts exult and triumph in it? This is the true Philofopher's ftone, the divine magic of love which conveys all things into our hands, giving us a poffeffion and ufe in them of which nothing can deprive us.

By virtue of this, (as Paul juftly obferves) *" Being forrowful we yet always " rejoice ; having nothing we yet poffefs all " things."* Neither is this property in our neighbour's goods merely imaginary, but real and fubftantial; indeed, for more real to the true lover of men, than it is generally to the legal owners of them. For how is property in things otherwife to be confidered than by the

satisfaction

satisfaction which they yield to the presumed owner? And if the benevolent man find this satisfaction in them, and in a high degree, why are they not truly his? May not the tree with some degree of propriety be called yours if you can pluck and enjoy its fruits at pleasure? Nay, does not the propriety more truly belong to you, if you equally enjoy the benefit, without partaking the trouble and expence which fall on the real owner? A loving man therefore can never be poor or miserable, except all the world should come to want and distress, for while his neighbour has any thing, he will enjoy it—" *rejoicing with* " *those who rejoice.*"

BUT love not only advances us to the highest pitch of happiness attainable in this life, but, like a true friend, it will accompany us into heaven, and there complete our felicity, by exalting us us to the society of "*angels and spirits of just men made perfect.*"

Among all the nations of the earth, the pleasing persuasion has prevailed, that the souls of good men shall pass away after death into brighter climes than these, where assembled in the sweetest society, they shall enjoy pleasures which were never permitted them to taste in this vale of tears.

This strongest and dearest sentiment of nature, is confirmed by revelation, which assures us, that heaven, the city of the eternal King, is inhabited by a great multitude, which no man can number, composed of all the wise and good that ever existed in the universe of God; and who, now separated from every infirmity, dwell together in the dearest amity and peace.

Desireable indeed must an access to such a society appear to us, who dwell in these abodes of frail humanity, whose whofe paffions are fo much at variance with our repofe! This man wounds us by a mortifying neglect, that infults us with fcorn and contempt. A third cruelly envies our felicity. A fourth inhumanly flanders our good name. And a fifth goes to law with us for our eftate. While thofe few who love us, often add to our uneafinefs by their follies or vices. Who would not leave fuch a wretched fociety as this, and gladly go to mingle with thofe bleffed friends, who can no more be miferable themfelves, nor render us fo? Where every countenance will fhine upon us with fmiles of undiffembled affection; and every eye will beam unutterable love? Where mighty angels will be as endearingly attentive to us, as fondeft bretheren; while heavenly fages will pour forth the treafures of their wifdom to entertain us, though the feebleft of faints?

But, alas! is it for us whose hearts are defiled, and who drink in iniquity like water, to be numbered with these children of God, and to have our lot among such saints? Yes it is. For though the precious gold of Ophir could not purchase such high honors for us; and though rocks of proffered diamonds would not be received in exchange; yet there is a power, a secret charm, that can open for us the everlasting doors, and admit us into those courts of glory. That charm is Love, which, by exercising every odious passion, and adorning us with its own celestial graces, will secure our welcome, and render us dear to every saint in paradise. And were it not for love, which thus refines our nature, and transforms us into angels of light, never could we mingle in the society of those heavenly lovers.

"Birds

"Birds of a feather flock toge-ther."—As gentle doves, who delight in mutual careffes, fly on wings of terror, from thofe birds whofe fiery eyes threaten hateful ftrife; fo angels of love, muft retire with as natural an abhorrence, from the fociety of dark and malignant fpirits. Between no two things in nature, does there exift fo irreconcilable an oppofition, as between love and hatred. Water and oil—fire and fnow, may, by the powerful arts of chemiftry, be taught to forget their native antipathies, and to rufh together into friendly embraces: But by no arts can tender-hearted love be brought to look with complacency on any appearance of hatred and mifery. And the more ardent our love, the more exquifite will be our diftrefs, at the view of fuch fcenes.

Philander, whofe life is a feries of beneficence that reflects honor on human

man nature, was, during the earlier part of his days, strangely fond of that most vulgar practice, boxing. But happening to read Dr. Blair's sermon on gentleness, he was brought to see so clearly, the beauty and blessedness of a benevolent temper, that he has ever since cultivated it as the brightest ornament, and highest happiness of his life. Philander often now observes to his friends, that nothing surprises him more than the difference which he finds between the feelings, of the present and past periods of his life. That formerly, when a stranger to love, the sight of a battle was *matter of fun* to him; and a broken head, or a bloody nose, a mere bagatelle, *quite a trifle*. But that now, were he compelled to see two men striving in battle, and with furious countenances and eyes darting hatred, inflicting cruel blows on each other, he verily believes it would harrow up his soul

and

and fill him with infupportable horror. And fuch, I am confident, would be the feelings of every truly benevolent heart. Now, if we who are but babes in love, and whofe hearts ftill retain much of their former hardnefs and infenfibility, are, notwithftanding, fo fhocked at the fight of bad paffions; how much more would the bleffed angels, thofe pure fpirits of love, be fhocked at the fight of fuch things? Hence, it clearly appears, that were God to throw open the gates of heaven, and to invite us to enter with all our pride, haughtinefs, fcorn, envy and hatred about us; fo far from being welcome to the angels, we fhould turn their heaven into hell. It would grieve their generous bofoms, to fee us fo completely damned; and it would equally fhock their feelings to fee us fo perfectly loathfome and abominable; and they would, no doubt, prefer their joint petitions to God, for permiffion to retire into some other part of his dominions, where, far removed from such disquieting scenes, they might renew their joys in contemplating the beauty of each others virtues, and in rejoicing in the greatness of their mutual bliss. Would we therefore gain a welcome admission into those blest abodes, where angels and the youngest sons of light, spend their blissful days in joys unknown to mortal sense—Let us Love. This is the darling attribute of God; "*For God is love.*" And this is the grace that gives to ministering spirits all their surpassing joys and glories. Washed in this heavenly Jordan, the foulest leper becomes fresher than the new-born babe. Bathed in this divine Bethesda, the blackest heart and most malevolent spirit becomes whiter than snow. Mark the glorious change. His eyes, lately glaring with infernal fires, now emit the softest beams of benevolence. His cheeks

cheeks, once pale with envy, now bloom with the rofy-red of joy. His countenance, e'er while dark with angry paffions, now wear the opening radiance of friendfhip. His voice, lately broken and difcordant with rage, is now fweeter than mufic; his heart, once the den of poifonous adders, is now the abode of gentleft affection; and he who fome time ago was the terror or hatred of all who knew him, is now become the delight of each eye and joy of every heart. His admiring friends, view him with tranfport as a dear monument of the mighty power of love; while holy angels welcome him with fweeteft fymphonies, and fill the eternal regions with acclamations of joy. *"Behold, this our brother was loft, but is found, he was dead, but is alive."*

AND though on our firft entrance into the company of bleffed angels, we cannot be half fo loving and lovely as they

they are, yet will not this diminish their affection for us; for, clearly perceiving, that though but babes, we yet possess the fair features and precious qualities of godlike souls, they will cordially love and tenderly embrace us, as their younger brethren, and as infant angels. While meeting with no cruel obstructions to our love, as in this world, but on the contrary, finding ourselves beloved and caressed by each saint and angel, we shall daily become more grateful and affectionate, and consequently more lovely in the eyes, and more dear to the hearts, of those blessed people. And now, what words can express, what fancy can conceive the various and exquisite pleasures, that we may expect to meet with, in so wise, so all-accomplished and endearing a society? If the conversation of *great* and *good natured wits*, be so highly entertaining, that men of taste would give any thing to spend an evening

ing with a party of such; how much more desireable must it be to spend an eternity in the company of angels? For, as in point of knowledge, wit, and eloquence, they must be far superior to the brightest geniuses of our world, and incomparably more affectionate, they cannot but make the most delightful company. From the vast stores of their wisdom and experience, they can easily draw an almost infinite variety of the most entertaining topics, on which such good and gentle spirits, will not fail to converse in the most free and endearing manner. Then, what a heavenly conversation must theirs be, whose scope is the most glorious knowledge, and its law the most perfect friendship?

Who would not willingly leave a childish, forward and ill natured world, for the blessed society of those wise friends and perfect lovers? And what a felicity must it be to spend an eternity, in such a noble a noble converſation? Where we ſhall hear the deep philoſophy of heaven communicated with mutual freedom, in the wiſe and amiable diſcourſes of angels, and of glorified ſpirits, who, without any reſerve or affectation of myſtery, without paſſion or peeviſh contention for victory, do freely philoſophize and impart the treaſures of each others knowledge? For ſince all ſaints there are great philoſophers, and all philoſophers perfectly ſaints, we may conclude, that knowledge and goodneſs, wiſdom and love, will be moſt charmingly intermixed throughout all their converſation, and render it delightful in the higheſt degree. When therefore we ſhall leave this vain and unſociable world, and on our landing on the ſhores of eternity, ſhall be met by all our good old friends, who are gone to heaven before us, and who now with infinite joy for our ſafe arrival, receive and conduct us into the

ſplendid

splendid society of all the good and generous souls, who ever lived in the world: when we shall be familiar friends with angels and archangels; and all the shining courtiers of heaven shall call us bretheren, and welcome us into their glorious society, with all the tender endearments and caresses, of those heavenly lovers, O how will all these mighty honors and joys, swell our bosoms with tides of transport almost too big to bear!

But love not only renders us thus happy, by adorning us with such graces as give us a hearty welcome to the society, and joys of angels; but, O godlike power of charity! it even enables us to make all their joys our own.

It is a natural property of love, when sincere, to unite so closely the hearts o lovers, as to make their interests common, and thus to render the joys of the one, the joys of the other. Every man carries in his own bosom a proof of this

this delightful truth. Do not the virtues of a dear brother, give us as exquisite joy, as if we ourselves were adorned with them? Have not the high commendations bestowed on a beloved sister, thrilled through our hearts, in as pure streams of pleasure as if we ourselves had been the honored subject of them? Now, if love, which is a native of heaven, produces, even in the cold soil of the human heart, such *delicious fruits of joy* at the sight of our neighbour's happiness, how much more copious and exquisite must be its growth and flavour, when restored to heaven, it enjoys all the energies of its native soil and climate? If therefore, while here on earth, we make such progress in brotherly love, as to relish our neighbour's happiness as our own, " *heartily rejoicing with him when he rejoices;*" we may rest assured, that on going to heaven, and entering into the society of blessed angels

angels, we shall find the joys of congratulating love, far superior to what we ever experienced in this world. With what sacred delight shall our hearts overflow, when, on opening our eyes in those blissful mansions, we behold around us, such bright bands of glorious beings? The sight of these lovely and happy people, will open new springs of joy in our bosoms. With what wonder, love, and praise, shall we contemplate that hand which drew such magnificent scenes; these streets paved with gold, these gorgeous palaces hewn from diamond quarries, these walls flaming with the stones of heaven, these rivers flowing with liquid silver, these fields decked with immortal flowers, these sacred shades formed by the trees of God; and which, after having cloathed these regions in such godlike splendors, raised up so many myriads of glorious beings to inhabit them forever? There, among those favoured spirits, we shall meet with none of those melancholy scenes which here so often embitter our lives. Here, the strong pains and cries of those whom we love, often wring our hearts and call tears of bitterest sorrow from our eyes; but there, God shall wipe all tears from our eyes, and pain and sickness are unknown. Here, the pale cheek, the hollow eye, and trembling voice of languishing friends, often sicken our hearts, and press our spirits to the earth; but there, health blooms with freshest roses on each immortal cheek, and imparts a vigor that shall never know decay. Here, we often behold our dearest relatives struggling in the agonies of death, and hear, with stupifying grief, their last expiring groans; but there, among those holy angels, death never shewed his ghastly countenance, and their glorified bodies are deathless as the eternal Jehovah.

Now

Now, what words can expreſs the joys of thoſe bleſſed people, who love each other with a tenderneſs unknown to mortal boſoms, and whoſe love is continually feaſted with the view of each others happineſs, a happineſs which no time can terminate, and which neither man nor devil can impair! For perfect lovers have all their joys and griefs in common between them; but the heavenly lovers having no griefs among them, do only communicate their joys to one another. And where they love ſo perfectly as they do in heaven, there can be no ſuch thing as a private or particular happineſs, but every one *muſt* have a ſhare in that of every one, and conſequently in this, their mutual communication of joys, every one's happineſs, will, by his friendſhip to every one, be multiplied into as many happineſſes as there are ſaints and angels in heaven; and thus, every joy, of every member of the church triumphant, runs round the whole body, in an eternal circulation. For that bleſſed body being all compoſed of conſenting hearts, that, like perfect uniſons, are tuned up to the ſame key, when any *one* is touched, *every one* echoes, and refounds the ſame note: and while they thus mutually ſtrike upon each other, and all are affected with every one's joys, it is impoſſible, but, that in a ſtate where there is nothing but joy, there ſhould be a continual concert of raviſhing harmony among them. For ſuch is their dear concern for one another, that every one's joy not only pays to, but receives tribute from the joy of every one: ſo that when any one bleſſed ſpirit rejoices, his joy goes round the whole ſociety, and then all their rejoicings in his joy, reflow upon, and ſwell and multiply it; and ſo as they thus cordially borrow each others joys, they always pay them back

back with intereſt, and by thus reciprocating, do everlaſtingly increaſe them. And now, what unſpeakable rejoicing and congratulations will there be among us, when we ſhall paſs all heaven over, through ten thouſand millions of bleſſed beings, and meet none but ſuch as we moſt dearly love, and are as dearly beloved by? eſpecially when we ſhall find no defect either of goodneſs, or happineſs in them, nor they in us, to damp our mutual joy and delight, but every one ſhall be what every one wiſhes him— a perfect and bleſſed friend.

WHAT eternal thanks do we not owe to the author of all good, for giving us ſouls that are capable of aſcending to the ſociety of theſe glorious beings, and of participating forever in their exalted delights? And how muſt it inflame our gratitude to him for appointing LOVE to be the golden road leading to thoſe celeſtial regions, and for employing ſo many arguments, and taking, if we may thus speak, so much pains to persuade us to walk in it? For, take all the laws of God, whether written on hearts of flesh, or tables of stone, or on softer leaves of evangelic paper, and cast them up—What is their amount? Love.— *Love is the bond of perfection. Love is the fulfilling of the law. He hath shewed thee, O man! what is good, and what doth the Lord thy God require of thee but to love him, thy Parent God, with all thy heart, and thy neighbour as thyself.*

And as God has thus enjoined love, so has he disposed every thing in an order the most favourable to the production of it.

For who is this neighbour whom we are enjoined to love? Is he some vile inferior creature whom it were hard, if not impossible to love? No, he is, on the coutrary, a most noble being, and descended from the greatest family in the

the universe. He is no less a personage, than a young prince, a son of the Great King eternal, whom he is not only allowed but even commanded to call *his* father. If some young nobleman cloathed in silks and broad-cloaths, scented with rich perfumes, and richly equipaged, were to call at our houses, we should instantly be impressed with sentiments of respect, and good will for him, and readily invite him to the hospitalities of our tables. But what are silver and gold? what are silks and broad-cloths? what are fine horses and servants? in comparison of that immortal soul which this neighbour possesses, and those eternal beauties of which his soul is capable? know, that he was made but *a few degrees lower than the angels*, and that God, the true judge of merit, has, on account of the rich excellencies of his nature, created this world, with all the goodly brightness

ness of heaven, and all the costly furniture of earth, to serve him.

"*Thou madest him to have dominion over the works of thy hands; thou hast put all things under his feet.*"

He possesses a soul capable of so *exceedingly great and eternal a weight of glory*, that rather than he should be deprived of it forever by sin, God himself came down on earth to expiate it, and by his own most perfect and amiable life and lessons, to allure him back to love heaven. God has adopted him as his son, and made him a free denizen of his heavenly city; and has appointed his own glorious angels to wait on him, as on the heir of salvation and candidate for eternal glory. Can we then think it hard to love him whom God thus loves and thus delights to honor?

But if it be easy to love a person of eminent dignity and excellence, it becomes easier and pleasanter still to love him,

him, if he be a near kinfman and friend. Well, this is truly the cafe betwixt our neighbour and us. He is our near relation—our brother—bone of our bone, and flefh of our flefh. God kindly raifed him up to be unto us as a companion and a help-mate, to lighten our burdens, to multiply our comforts, and, like dear *children walking in love,* to enjoy together the rich fruits of our mutual induftry, rejoicing in the prefent bounties of our common parent, and exulting in the hopes of better yet to come.

AND as if all thefe tender and endearing circumftances were not fufficient, God himfelf has put forth his hand, and touched our hearts with fentiments of good will towards each other.

THESE native fentiments of love, thefe dear remains of God's own image, originally ftamped on our minds, appear very vifible in all, even in thofe unfortunates, whofe whose hard lot and corrupting companions have done much to stifle them.

Take you poorest of men! who gleans precarious and scanty bread, by hard and humble toil. His four looks and crabbed manners give room to suspect that he is a misanthrope, an utter stranger to *natural affection;* but the slightest experiment will soon discover what tender sympathies unite him to his kind.

You need not tell him of flourishing cities, with all their gay inhabitants, swallowed up by the devouring sword, or ruthless flames, while mourning millions loaded with chains, are driven far from their native homes to make room for new masters. No; such horrid tragedies are not necessary to touch the springs of his compassion. Let him but hear the song of Chevy Chase, or the tender ballad of the Babes in the Wood; or carry him to the Theatre, and let him

him hear, though but in a play, in mere fiction, the story of poor Barnwell, let him behold that unfortunate young man, who set out in life adorned with comely virtues, and the darling of all who knew him; but soon alas! too soon, arrested by a beauteous harlot, he falls an easy prey to her wiles, is stript of all his virtues and honors, and betrayed into crimes for which he dies on the ignominious gallows.—'Tis enough, this simple tale of woe calls up all his feelings of generous distress, and bathes his cheeks in floods of sympathetic tears.

Does not this our ready disposition to suffer with our suffering neighbour, and to *weep with him when he weeps*, plainly prove how much God has done to make it easy for us to love one another. To this he has added another charming evidence, I mean the inexpressible joy which he infuses into our hearts,

hearts on doing works of love to the neceffitous.

"Pray fir," faid a young Virginian to his friend, " on what act of your " life do you reflect with the higheft " complacency?" " Why fir," replied the other, " happening to hear that an " old flave of my father's was fick, I went " up to his quarter to fee him. On enqui-
" ry, I found, that in confequence of his " extreme age, and inability to render " further fervices in the crop, he was " cruelly neglected by the overfeer, and " often made to fuffer for a meal of vic-
" tuals. Blufhing to find that this was " the principal caufe of his prefent in-
" difpofition, I inftantly returned, and " taking a negro lad, carried up a flitch " of bacon, a loaf of bread, and a peck " of meal. On feeing the prefent which " I had brought him, his half-famifhed " nature revived, and a fudden gufh " of tears trickled down his cheeks.

" Lifting

"Lifting up his eyes, he gave me such a look of gratitude and love, as pierced my very soul, and kindled a pleasure, which time, instead of diminishing, does but increase!"

The pleasures which we find in eating and drinking, we gratefully consider as given by the Creator, to attach us to those refreshments so necessary to life. With equal wisdom and gratitude, let us remember that the heartfelt delight which accompanies and succeeds our deeds of love, were meant to allure us to cherish that divine affection which is *better than life*.

For the same benevolent purpose, the author of our being is pleased to exert on us the whole force of another powerful spring of action; I mean interest. Our dearest interests in this world are best promoted, by maintaining a loving correspondence with our neighbours. So uncertain is our condition, so liable are we all to the changes and chances of this mortal life, that no man can tell how soon he may owe his very life and fortune to the gratitude of a poor neighbour or slave who loves him. How many accounts have we heard of poor negroes, whose love for a good master has made them bravely to step in betwixt him and danger; sometimes, like faithful spaniels, plunging in, and drawing him out of deep waters, where he was in the very act of drowning? Sometimes, like Salamanders, rushing upon and extinguishing furious fires, that were destroying his houses, and perhaps half the labours of his life? And sometimes, like Hectors, fighting with desperate courage in his defence, when attacked, and in danger of being severely beaten and killed by his enemies?

But love not only thus marshals *an army with banners* around us for our safety;

safety; it also pours a sweet sunshine of peace and harmony over our days.

St. Paul, who was a much safer guide in matters of *religion*, than Mr. Paine, advises us to *walk in love with our neighbours, if we would lead a quiet and peaceable life.* For as men naturally perceive a fragrance in the rose, and a sweetness in the honey-comb; so naturally do they discern a heavenly charm and beauty in love. Adorned therefore with the friendly dispositions, the fair dealings, and gentle manners of this divine passion, we shall not fail to find favour in the eyes of our neighbours, and to be beloved and caressed by them. Hence we walk among them as among brothers, in every face we see a friendly smile, at every house a hearty welcome, never devising any mischief against them, we never dream of their devising any against us. Our hearts are now at rest, our countenances are serene, our voices melodious,

melodious, our manners mild, our sleep sweet, and our whole life quiet and peaceable: And, as a blessed consequence of all this, together with the highest enjoyment of the present life, we are in the best frame of mind to prepare ourselves for that which is to come. Happily freed from the anxiety and vexation of all bad passions, we profitably contemplate our numberless obligations to love God and one another, and thus, in the multitude of our good thoughts, daily grow in virtue and piety.

But all this goodly Canaan, this land of love, flowing with richest milk and honey of peace, is snatched from our eyes by the demon-hand of hatred, and nought appears in its place but a land of darkness and of death, whose streams are of gall, and its fruits of bitter ashes.

By over-reaching a neighbour in a bargain (which we shall be too apt to do if we love him not), we make him

our

our enemy. Perhaps he has the spirit to tell us of our baseness to our faces, or to talk of it behind our backs. This fires our bosoms with odious and painful passions. Challenges or law-suits, with all their ignominious vexations, hurtful, and often fatal consequences, ensue.

Or by treating him with unreasonable severity (a thing very feasible if we love him not), we enflame his resentment to such an height, that not content with stabbing our reputation, he threatens our property and lives. Our curses now multiply thick and fast upon our heads. We can no longer sleep in quiet, from dread of having our houses fired over our heads. We are actually afraid (the memory of those who read may help them to instances) to stir out, or, like people in the neighbourhood of hostile Indians, must make our visits with pistols in our pockets, and carabines in our hands.

Thus, through defect of love, we are often dragged upon the stage against our wills, and there made to act parts in tragedies, which neither become nor please us. Our thoughts taken off from all delightful subjects, are turned to solicitous cares of self-preservation and defence. Our minds are discomposed by vexatious passions. Our credit is blasted by false reports and slanderous defamations. Our hearts are kept continually boiling with choler, our faces over-clouded with discontent, our ears filled with discordant noises of contradiction, clamor and reproach; and our whole frame of body and soul distempered with the worst of passions. In the meantime our natural rest is disturbed, our necessary business is hindred, our happiness in this life is utterly wretched and lost, and the great concerns of heaven and eternal

eternal glory are entirely laid afide. O how much better it is to walk in the fmooth and flowery paths of love, than thus to wander in the rugged ways of hatred, overgrown with briars, and befet with fnares; to fail gently down the courfe of life on the filver current of friendfhip, than to be toffed on the tempeftuous fea of contention; to behold the lovely face of heaven fmiling with a cheerful ferenity, than to fee it frowning with clouds or raging with ftorms! How much a peaceful ftate refembles heaven, into which no ftrife nor clamor ever enter, but where bleffed fouls converfe together in perfect love, and perpetual concord! And how a condition of enmity refembles hell, that black and difmal region of dark hatred, fiery wrath, and horrible tumult! How like a paradife the world would be flourifhing in joy and reft, if men would but cheerfully confpire in love, and generoufly

nerously contribute to each others good: and how like a savage wildness it now is, when like wild beasts, they vex and persecute, worry and devour each other.

And to conclude, let us remember, that " *Love shall never fail,*" and that, the man of love " *shall be had in everlasting remembrance, and his memory shall be blessed.*" No spices can so embalm a man, no monument can so preserve his name, as works of love. The renown of power, of wit, and of learning, may rest on the minds of men with some admiration ; but the remembrance of love reigns in their hearts with sincerest affection, there erecting trophies triumphant over death, and oblivion. The good man's very dust is fragrant, and his grave venerable. His name is never mentioned without the tribute of a sigh, and loud acclamations of praise. And even when he is gone hence, and in person

son is no more seen, he remains visible in the footsteps and fruits of his goodness. The poor man beholds him in the comfortable subsistence which he still receives from his bounty. The sick man feels him in the refreshments which he yet enjoys from his charity. He survives in the hearts of the afflicted, who still remember the services which he rendered them so cheerfully. And his weeping friends dry up their tears when they think of his virtues, the rich fruits of which they doubt not, he is now enjoying in a better world. *His memory shall likewise endure forever*, in the favor of God, and in those glorious rewards which he will bestow upon him for his love to his brethren. *God will not forget his labour of love*, but will raise him up after the short slumbers of the grave, to receive that unfading crown, and that precious pearl of eternal life:—
" *Well done good and faithful servant,—I was*

was hungry and you gave me food, I was thirsty and you gave me drink, naked was I and you cloathed me, sick and in prison and you visited me, enter now into the joy of your lord."

Thus, when all the flashes of sensual pleasure are quite extinct; when all the flowers of secular glory are withered away; when all earthly treasures are buried in darkness; when this world with all its fashions are utterly vanished and gone, the good man's state will be still firm and flourishing, *and his righteousness shall endure for ever.*

If then you would be happy indeed; happy in every condition, and in the discharge of every duty; happy in life and in death; happy in this world and in that which is to come; learn to Love.

" This having learnt, thou hast at-
" tained the sum of wisdom. Hope no
" higher, though all the stars thou
" knowest

"knowest by name, and all the etherial "powers; all secrets of the deep; all "nature's works, or works of God in "heaven, earth, air, or sea; and all "the riches of this world enjoyedst, "and all that rule one empire. Only "add deeds to thy knowledge answer- "able. Add faith, add virtue, patience, "temperance; add LOVE, the soul of "all the rest; then shall thou not be "loath to leave this world, but shalt in- "herit a world that's happier far."

MILTON.

F I N I S.

www.ingramcontent.com/pod-product-compliance
Lightning Source LLC
Chambersburg PA
CBHW030739230426
43667CB00007B/773